BIGGER THAN DIVORCE

BIGGER THAN DIVORCE

A Muslim Woman's Path to Healing and Purpose

Makeda Yasenlul

BUKAYA
PUBLICATIONS

 BUKAYA
PUBLICATIONS

For inquiries, collaborations, or bulk order requests, please contact: makeda@makedayasenlul.com

ISBN: 979-8-9926282-0-3

Library of Congress Control Number: 2025902729

To Mamasha and Nura,
who give so much and love unconditionally

بسم الله والصلاة والسلام على رسول الله

CONTENTS

INTRODUCTION

The Stanley Mosk Courthouse in Los Angeles County has witnessed two of the defining moments of my life. The first time I walked through its doors, I felt the energy of possibility. The building's marble columns, rising high and grand, seemed to mirror my own ambition. I was there to claim my dream job; I was stepping into a role I'd worked years to achieve. My stride was sure, my gaze steady.

The second time, those same doors loomed like a judgment, heavy and imposing. The high ceilings and echoing halls pressed down on me as I slipped my badge into my pocket, barely looking up, hoping not to meet anyone's eyes. This time, I wasn't there for a job but to file for divorce. A different kind of finality waited behind those doors. I looked around nervously, praying I wouldn't see anyone I knew. This was the beginning of my end, and I did not want witnesses.

In the weeks and months that followed, instead of turning to people for support, I turned inward—to solitude, and to the quiet comfort of zaatar bread.

Right around the time I filed for divorce, I was going through a zaatar bread phase. I would enjoy the tangy, earthy treat after Fajr every day with a hot cup of coffee. This was the only time of day when I had the privacy I needed to rage and to grieve. So as I ate my breakfast, I contemplated. I cried. I seethed. Zaatar bread was with me when I shook from anger. It was there as I hid the sound of my sobs from my daughter and mother. It was there when I started to put the pieces of myself back together. After that time, I didn't have zaatar bread for a long time.

A few months ago, I had the opportunity to have some zaatar bread, and something strange happened. With the first bite, a flood of emotions hit me. It was the pain and misery and grief and rage of that earlier time. It was only then that I realized how very far I had come. To my amazement, that lost, mad woman was gone. I was a new woman.

Allah ﷻ constantly sends us signs and wake-up calls. It is up to us to nurture our connection to Him, pay attention, and extract the lessons. In 2020 and 2021, when divorce turned my world upside down, I found myself submerged in a deeply contemplative and soul-searching journey. It was a time when all sorts of feelings surfaced, and it felt as if I was meeting myself for the first time. I had what Brené Brown might call a "~~breakdown~~ spiritual awakening"—I stopped pressing the snooze button on my life and finally woke up to a deep exploration of myself and a commitment to live intentionally.

Why Did I Write This Book?

Wandering through a Barnes & Noble bookstore one day, a book caught my eye. The title promised that it would teach me how to be an amazing and financially independent single mom. I was gagging within a few minutes of flipping through the book: The advice was such a violation of my values that I couldn't make it past the first few pages. The lessons disregarded any notion of a Creator.

This seemingly small encounter with that book gave me an idea. Even though I was an avid reader, I had not even thought to check if a book could help me process my divorce. In the days that followed, I looked for an Islamic book about divorce that could give me solace. I expected to find a plethora of books dedicated to every facet of this painful experience. Divorce and domestic violence. Divorcing as a senior. Divorce and infertility. I scoured Islamic bookstores. I searched online. I asked people for recommendations. Would you believe that I could not find a single book about how to handle divorce from an Islamic perspective? If one exists, it must be obscure enough that it doesn't appear in online searches and no one seems to know about it. I searched high and low for such a book and simply could not find one.

Close to 50 percent of marriages today will end in either divorce or permanent separation, and this trend extends into the Muslim community. According to Imam Mohamed Magid, Executive Director of the All-Dulles Area Muslim Society (ADAMS) Center, the community has seen "an increase in divorce from people married for a while and those married for a short time." Some of us don't need data to tell us how rampant divorce is in our community; we witness it among our friends and family.

The *Oxford Dictionary* defines divorce as "the legal ending of a marriage." The *Merriam-Webster Dictionary* says it is "to legally dissolve one's marriage with (one's spouse)." The dictionary *doesn't* mention the emotional, social, physical, and legal challenges one goes through when ending a marriage, while simultaneously figuring out how to move forward in life.

Despite the glaringly difficult reality of divorce, we seem to remain profoundly silent when it comes to offering advice about it. We do not hear divorcees talking about their experience. We do not find guidance on how to avoid divorce or heal from it. We do not see conversations about the reality of life after divorce. There is a huge gap between the prevalence of divorce and the scarcity in people addressing it.

After a few months, I decided I needed to stop complaining and be someone who steps up. That was when I started documenting my journey and the lessons I had learned along the way.

In this book, I share my journey from being an angry, lost woman with no self-worth to someone who found emotional healing, gained wisdom from her divorce, and now lives with purpose.

Part One, "Lost," lays the foundation for my story. Together, we will begin the grief process and discover who we truly are. Part Two, "Finding the Path," introduces key mindset shifts to aid in moving on from divorce. Part Three, "Embracing the Journey," provides practical tips for thriving in your new postdivorce era.

Please consider me your sister. I will walk with you as you figure out your own journey. Bear in mind that this book does not aim to address issues related to domestic violence or other forms of extreme abuse. It is drawn from my experience and perspective: I was not married for long, I never left my home, and I have a young daughter. As such, what you find here may or may not be relevant to your situation.

How to Get the Most Out of This Book

I recommend that you approach this book thoughtfully and that you take time to reflect and allow the lessons to seep in along the way. You may feel defensive about some of the advice you find in this book. Sometimes we are not ready to hear things, and it may make us angry when we do. That's OK. You won't always be stuck in that stage. A well-intentioned word of advice will make sense when it is supposed to. Just recognize that it is possible you are not ready to hear that particular bit of advice, file it away, and revisit it later.

I don't want you just reading either. I want you to dig deep and take action that leads to real change in your life. That's why I've included reflective questions throughout the book. You'll find them placed where they fit best—within the chapters or at the end of the chapters as challenge questions. These aren't just questions to reflect on—they are designed to push you toward clarity and growth. It's also a space for you to articulate your deepest thoughts and track your progress over time.

For your convenience, all the questions are also compiled into a digital workbook, which you can print and use to keep all your answers organized in one place. You can find it at https://www.makedayasenlul.com/divorcebookresources.

Kintsugi is a Japanese art form that repurposes broken pottery. Instead of painting over the cracks, hiding them or discarding the pottery altogether, the artist joins the pieces together and illuminates the cracks using gold. Kintsugi literally translates as "golden joinery." The flaw ends up making the piece more beautiful.

I want this beautiful healing for each of us: to turn the chapter of our life that once broke us into a beautiful experience that we highlight. It's now a part of who we are, etched into our story in this existence. We won't conceal it. Instead, we'll embrace these changes and use them as a catalyst to become better than ever. However tough your journey may get, remember that Allah ﷻ is always with you.

Let the journey to hope and inner peace begin.

Part One
_____

LOST

1

Broken by Divorce

It wasn't meant to be this way.

I was approaching thirty—a significant deadline—and I found myself frantically searching for a spouse. My twenty-eighth and twenty-ninth years were spent thinking about marriage day in and day out. Every man I met was quickly assessed for his potential as a husband, from the grocery store clerk who said "assalamu alaikum" to the bearded biker with a pet snake in his profile picture.

My fears were deep-seated.

One memory in particular stood out. I was no more than ten years old, sitting with my aunt, my sister, and an older cousin in the living room of my childhood home. My cousin had recently turned thirty and was unmarried at the time. Aunty asked the dreaded question: "Are there any potential prospects you are considering for marriage?" The air filled with tension.

The answer was no.

My aunt continued, "Well, you just turned thirty—you've expired. I don't think you will find anyone now."

My cousin burst into tears and ran out of the room.

I never forgot that exchange. I could not wrap my head around how humans could "expire." Like the eggs I carefully inspected before buying at the local souk.

———

When I was around seven, I remember playing my favorite game of pretend with the neighborhood kids. It was my wedding, and I was so excited and happy, prancing around with my imaginary veil on my head, making sure the rocks on leaves (food for the guests, of course!) were served to every child.

From a young age, we dream about our wedding, the husband we will have, what our children will look like, and the life we will lead. As the years pass, we hold on to these desires subconsciously. If things end up differently, we are not only dealing with the loss of what we had but also with the loss of what could have been.

In my language, Amharic, there is a derogatory term for people who end up not marrying: *komo ker*. It carries the connotation that this person is unwanted by anyone. In a culture where marriage is seen as the definition of what makes a woman whole, I approached the prospect of getting married or not as a life-or-death situation. Fortunately, I would evade death.

———

I grew up in Ethiopia, in a family that was always busy—not with social events or technology, but with the daily grind of chores and

10

school. Education was held in the highest regard. Our mission was simple and clear: Get good grades, then get a good job, then get married and have kids.

At twenty-three, I moved to the United States. The next several years were a blur of trying to find my footing in a new country. I spent those years waiting tables and doing other odd jobs, deeply ashamed that I had failed in life. I had fallen short of the first thing that had been drilled into me: Succeed academically and secure a highly paid, respectable career.

Then, I met *him*. He was funny and well-read, and nothing else seemed to matter—not even the fact that he had recently gone through a divorce. Out of respect for both of us, I won't dwell on the specifics of our marriage. But I will say that the marriage lasted all of eleven months.

At the end, when the divorce was impending, with proceedings having already begun in court, I was confused. I had never even moved out of my home. My spouse still lived in another state—we had been in the process of figuring out our living arrangements when the zaatar hit the fan, as it were. I was as worried about what people would say as I was about my future.

I was also scared of the new identity I would now have to embody: that of a *fet*. *Fet* is the term in my culture for divorcees, one that is meant to degrade and induce shame. *Fet*s are looked down upon and placed low in the social hierarchy, just as *komo ker*s are. I'd barely escaped one land mine, and here I was walking into another.

———

Short-lived as my marriage was, it completely changed my life. I was now a mother, raising a baby alone, all while dealing with a plethora of emotional wounds—old ones I didn't even know I had and some new ones for good measure.

During the litigation, I *looked* like I was functioning well: I continued to work, smile, and take care of my duties at home. My inner state was something else entirely. Rage, depression, and anxiety took turns fighting for control of my heart. And I *hated* him. The man I had been closest to, the one I had been intimate with in every sense, now felt like an enemy, a Trojan horse I should never have allowed into the inner sanctum of my heart or body.

I replayed hurtful conversations over and over in my mind, reopening the wounds afresh. I felt worthless as a human and scared for my daughter's future. Now she would grow up without a father around, and her father was a man I felt guilty for marrying in the first place, as if I had violated her right to a good father by not choosing wisely.

Most of all, I could not believe I was about to be one of *them*: the dreaded divorcees. Lonely women with worry lines on their foreheads, receiving no assistance but plenty of pity. What I didn't know then was that I would *have to* accept my new reality in order to grieve and start the healing process.

The Stages of Grief

Grief isn't limited to death. It is a necessary response to any significant loss, and it reshapes our lives in ways we may have never expected. There are five stages of grief: denial, anger, bargaining, depression, and acceptance.

Denial

For most people, the first reaction when experiencing a loss is denial. They go through a period of disbelief in which they find it difficult to accept their changing reality. Denial is useful because it slows the first wave of pain.

In cases of divorce, denial may take many forms, such as denying that they are headed toward a separation, downplaying the seriousness of the relationship issues, or romanticizing the past to evade emotional realities. Some may actively sidestep conversations about the divorce and continue routine activities as if unaffected.

Anger

After denial, most people jump into a state of anger. People may ask questions such as "Why did this happen?" They may direct their anger toward themselves, the person or thing they lost, or even Allah ﷻ.

During divorce, people may outwardly express their anger through confrontations or aggression. Some may internalize their anger, festering in resentment and blame or attempting to assign responsibility for the divorce. Some may seek justice or revenge.

Bargaining

This state of grief manifests itself in negotiations and internal dialogue that asks "What if?" and laments "If only I had." Bargaining also often manifests as bargaining with Allah ﷻ, where people make promises to do something in exchange for relief. During this stage, people are desperate to reduce the impact of the loss and regain what has been taken from them.

During divorce, bargaining can take various forms, such as promises of behavioral change, compromises in settlements, and last-ditch efforts like couples therapy to salvage the relationship. External interventions, such as involving friends or family, may also come into play.

Depression

In this stage, people start to face reality. They are beginning to understand how the loss will affect their life. Feelings of emptiness, sadness, and hopelessness start to present themselves.

In a divorce, the reality that has to be faced is the loss of the life one had always dreamed of. Fear of ending up alone forever can induce a sense of despair, which can be compounded by loneliness, guilt, and uncertainty about the future.

Acceptance

Acceptance is a beautiful stage in the process of grieving. Acceptance is when people start coming to terms with the reality of the loss and begin to find meaning in it. They start readjusting to life and their situation. There may not be complete closure, but there is a sense of readiness to live life again as best as they can. Finally, there is a sense of peace.

In the context of divorce, acceptance can look like the beginning of letting go. Though there is lingering pain, there is also emotional stability. The lessons start making sense. If there are children involved, the focus shifts to managing coparenting.

My dear sister, there is no way around the pain other than to feel the emotions you are experiencing and let them play out. Let the grieving process run its natural course. By knowing what to expect and understanding what you are going through, you will be better equipped to navigate the emotional roadblocks in a healthy way.

Remember that while the stages of grief listed above are a guide for identifying the different emotions you may experience, the grieving process is not linear. You may go through all the emotions at once, or one at a time, or several jumbled together. You will go back and forth. You may not go through some of the stages listed above. For example, some people may not feel anger, but only intense sadness and depression. The way each state is outwardly expressed can vary for everyone. Learning about these stages can help you understand your current state and catch a glimpse of what may be waiting ahead of you. Be kind to yourself as you navigate this process.

Back when my own pain and anger were fresh, I wish that someone had given me the words of advice that I will share with you now. Yes, there is healing on the other side, and you will get there, inshallah. But it is OK to hold on to your current pain for a little while. Feel it. Sit with it. Be still and process the pain, knowing that you can and will choose to move away from it toward healing, toward letting go.

It's OK to Be Angry

A therapist I was seeing in those early days told me, "It's OK to be pissed. You have the right to be angry, and the more you let yourself feel it, the more you can control it. Anger is paradoxical like that."

It is OK to be angry. In fact, it is part of the grieving process. Consider this the permission you need to feel anger.

I struggled with my anger because I felt like I was a bad Muslim for feeling angry and for being unable to feel forgiveness in my heart. But feeling anger does not make you a bad Muslim. What matters is how you choose to handle that anger.

I didn't know how to handle the merciless waves of red-hot rage that would suddenly hit me. I would be staring at a blank wall or washing dishes, and my face would twist with fury. I would compose scathing lines of prose that would rival the ancient sages of Arabia, and I would hit send on the texts. For a moment, I would feel satisfaction wash over me as I imagined my child's father feeling the burn. It lasted until the next wave hit, tempting me to release it all over again.

Deep down, I wanted him to validate me, validate my pain, and feel guilty. I wanted him to know how terrible he'd made me feel. What I didn't realize at the time was this: I still wanted to feel seen by him! It took a while to accept that he didn't need to acknowledge my pain. It was mine alone, and I needed to own it.

That's one of the reasons why it's important to cut all communications with your ex, except for practical arrangements and information about children. Otherwise, talking to him will open the door for more discussions that will just end up making you more upset. Accept that the two of you may never see eye to eye again, and you will have to go through this divorce without his input. No matter what you say, he will have his own thoughts and opinions. There is no need to straighten out the record with him because the records will not truly be straightened out!

When the Prophet (may peace be upon him; hereafter ﷺ) found a grieving mother at her child's grave, at her wit's end, he did not admonish her for her feelings. Rather, he advised the believers on behaving appropriately, no matter what their feelings are. We can and need to feel the pain: Take it to Allah (may He be glorified; hereafter ﷻ) and continue processing. You and I know that some pain is so great that we cannot even articulate it to ourselves, let alone share it with others. Only Allah ﷻ knows, and He doesn't need us to even speak the words aloud.

Anger and Backbiting

Sufyan ibn Abdullah (may Allah be pleased with him) reported: I said, "Oh Messenger of Allah, tell me of a matter I can depend upon?" The Messenger of Allah ﷺ said, "Say: My Lord is Allah. Then, remain upright." I said, "Oh Messenger of Allah, what do you fear most for me?" The Prophet pointed to his tongue and then he said, "This" (*Jami' al-Tirmidhi*).

Backbiting (*ghiba*) is speaking about someone in a way that they would dislike (for example, by mentioning their faults or shortcomings) without their knowledge.* Sometimes, you may be so hurt that it is easy to turn to gossip to ease the pain or vent your

---

*There are situations in which it is permissible for someone to reveal something unpleasant about someone else. For instance, it may be a warning for others or to tell an authority figure of a grievance. The scholars list cases where this is permissible.

anger. You may discuss your ex-husband with family and friends, sharing secrets he shared in confidence or calling him ugly names. You may also want validation and sympathy for all the pain. You may be looking for approval of your actions and decisions. However, realize that you don't need anyone to affirm your experiences. Your feelings are there for a reason and they are trying to tell you something. You don't need validation as permission to feel your feelings. Instead, you need to learn how to trust yourself.

Finding a healthy outlet to process your emotions, rather than discussing your ex with everyone else, is key here. For advice and input, only go to people who are mindful of Allah, can be impartial, and can give you sincere advice, not parrot what you want to hear. Backbiting will hurt you by increasing your sins and giving him your good deeds, which you definitely don't want to do!

Our families and friends can make things worse by adding fuel to the fire and engaging in backbiting as well. In the moment, it can feel validating to have others echo your own sentiments of hate and resentment; ultimately, however, none of this will help you or truly benefit you.

I was watching daytime TV once, and an audience member asked the TV host how to deal with her mom's anger with her dad. The questioner was an adult woman, whose mother and father had been divorced for almost twenty years, and her mother had spent that entire time consumed with anger toward her father. I couldn't believe that someone could hold on to so much anger for so long. I remember thinking, didn't she have a life of her own? At that time, I was quite naïve—I wasn't married yet.

Years later, after experiencing my own rage and the work it took (and still takes!) to move away from that anger, I feel a great deal of empathy for that woman on the long-ago TV show. I still don't want to be like her, and I don't want you to be like her either. The Messenger of Allah ﷺ told us that even a pinprick of pain that causes us to be patient is rewardable. He ﷺ said, "No fatigue, nor disease, nor sorrow, nor sadness, nor hurt, nor distress befalls a Muslim, even if it were the prick he receives from a thorn, but that Allah expiates some of his sins for that" (*Sahih al-Bukhari*). Our pain is not in vain. We are being rewarded for the hardships we are enduring. Allah ﷻ is always with us, closer to us than our jugular vein; He knows our deepest struggles.

Thoughts on Revenge and Justice

Heaven has no rage like love to hatred turned, nor hell a fury like a woman scorned. —William Congreve

In July 2011, Catherine Kieu cooked her husband dinner. It was to be his last meal with his penis intact. The dinner was laced with sleep medication.

The couple were having issues, and her husband had recently filed for divorce. When he went to sleep, Catherine tied his feet and arms to the bed and waited until he woke up. She then severed his penis with a knife and threw it in the garbage disposal. She was given a life sentence.

A quick google search will yield a plethora of gory results about lovers' revenge. Some may not be as brutal as Catherine's, but perfectly normal folks can find themselves doing outrageous things that no one would ever think they're capable of.

When we are rejected in love, our brains show activity in the regions linked with pain. The emotional pain is felt just as deeply as physical pain, if not more, because it is coupled with other feelings like rage.

> *Love's opposite is not hate, it is indifference.*
> *—Katherine Woodward Thomas*

So in the process of addressing wounds, be careful not to harm yourself further. When we are at our lowest, struggling with worthlessness and pain, the thought of delicious payback becomes more and more tempting. That is Shaytan preying on us in our most vulnerable moments, giving us "bright ideas." So be especially careful not to fall into haram while in the pursuit of justice. Revenge not only keeps wounds open, unnecessarily drawing out the pain, but it also deepens the damage to our souls.

During the time that I was processng my divorce and going through the stages of grief, my most defining emotion wasn't just anger—it was a furious blaze of rage. It was a rage that threatened to destroy. If I had the physical strength, I'm afraid of what I might have done if he were in front of me when he said something that angered me or triggered my rage.

Anger feels good. It makes us feel powerful, giving us a sense of validation. Yet this anger will not last forever; it will eventually fade away, even if it doesn't feel like it right now. Your goal should be to get to a place of looking at things dispassionately. Anger is not even a base emotion. It is pain, fear, or hurt beneath the surface that is showing up as anger. Pain needs to be felt, and if you don't allow yourself to experience pain, anger manifests in its place.

The need to get back at your ex for hurting you is born out of a desire to redress the wrong and achieve justice. Revenge will not accomplish this. If revenge won't redress the pain or bring you true justice, then what's the point in pursuing it?

Insisting on revenge is like picking at a scab so that it bleeds again and again. It's harder to hold back from scratching the itch and to let the scab heal completely, but it is necessary.

It's in your best interest to focus on moving forward and to remember that the greatest gift we can give ourselves is a pure heart. Don't waste your precious energy on things that will only worsen your pain. Tend to your wounds and make sure the pain isn't in vain by learning all the lessons it offers. Come back stronger and better than before!

Rest assured that this does not mean that any wrongs you've suffered will go unanswered for! Our *deen* (religion) firmly condemns oppression, as countless teachings remind us. The Prophet ﷺ narrated that Allah ﷻ said: "Oh my servants, I have forbidden oppression even for myself, and I have made it forbidden among you as well, so do not oppress one another" (*Sahih Muslim*).

Allah ﷻ hates injustice and transgression. Our teachers caution us more about the oppression we inflict on others than about the sins that only affect us. This is because Allah will not allow an oppressor of others to go without experiencing the consequences of it eventually, whether in this world or in the hereafter (or both!). On the other hand, He can and does forgive us easily for transgressions between ourselves and Him.

Rest assured that any transgression you suffered at the hands of your ex-husband will be dealt with fairly by Allah ﷻ, with every injustice your ex inflicted on you addressed. Allah is al-Hakam (the Judge), al-Muqsit (the Equitable), and al-Dayyan (the Supreme

Judge). Consider this verse, which strongly reinforces Allah's promise of absolute justice:

> *And We shall set up balances of justice on the Day of*
> *Resurrection, then none will be dealt with unjustly in anything.*
> *And if there be the weight of a mustard seed, We will bring*
> *it. And Sufficient are We to take account. (Qur'an 21:47)*

This verse describes Allah's meticulous fairness, promising that not even the tiniest deed will go unaccounted for. It provides reassurance that all injustices will be weighed with perfect precision.

A friend and I were discussing justice when she brought up the idea of "karma" and "what goes around comes around." The expressions we use to describe this idea haven't appeared out of thin air; they're rooted in centuries of people witnessing justice unfold. Who's to say you won't see victory in this life too? **Just make sure you're not the one meting it out, despite the temptation to make your ex feel the same pain he caused you**.

Being patient enough to leave the reckoning in Allah's hands is a challenge. Because of how difficult it is, I can only assume that the reward is double: one for the actual injustice and the other for the patience and faith it took to believe in the ultimate justice of Allah ﷻ. Trust Allah, and focus on being a good Muslim with a clear conscience.

CHALLENGE

As mentioned in the introduction, at the end of each chapter you will have the opportunity to answer reflection questions. As you work through your emotions and start your healing journey, please don't neglect this part. Be sure to take the time to answer the questions, preferably by hand. Seeing your words on paper is powerfully healing. Record your answers here or download the workbook at makedayasenlul.com/divorcebookresources.

Your challenge for this chapter is to assess your current values and emotional state. This will establish a foundation for your inner work as you move forward.

1. What does marriage mean to you?

2. Reflect on grief. What does your grief look like right now? What emotions are you experiencing?

3. How do these emotions manifest in your daily life?

4. It's OK to be angry, but it's not OK to take harmful actions based on anger. What are two healthy outlets that can help you cope with your anger?

2

Divorce and Stigma

One hadith haunts the sleepless nights of divorced Muslims and those who are contemplating divorce. They repeat it to themselves, weighed down by guilt:

> The Prophet ﷺ said, "Of all the lawful acts, the most detestable to Allah is divorce." (Abu Dawud)

Many of us have internalized ideas about how shameful divorce is. Our interpretations of the hadith above add to the social stigma, for both men and women. We see this hadith quoted to couples who are in situations that are clearly damaging to all parties involved, effectively guilt-tripping and spiritually blackmailing them to stay married.

However, most of us do not seek to learn the real meanings or context of ahadith; we don't even check our sources to authenticate the narrations. We do not explore and question the feelings of extreme guilt, doubt, and regret that are induced by the incorrect usage of these narrations. We do not seek to study the difference between cultural interpretations and the actual meanings and wisdoms behind narrations. Instead, we accept the negative judgment and live shrouded in shame, trapped in anguish as we question our choices and struggle against the heavy stigma surrounding divorce.

Let me be clear. As a divorcee who wants other divorcees to thrive, I am not advocating divorce as the first or only answer to marital issues.

We *should* be wary of divorce, as the hadith says. Divorce causes so much pain—for spouses, children, extended families, and society at large. Breaks in ties of kinship weaken society.

But does this mean that it is not acceptable to divorce, ever? Does this mean that it can't even be mandatory in some cases? Of course not. One look at our Islamic tradition is enough to confirm this. The Prophet ﷺ himself offered to divorce all his wives if they were unhappy, and Allah ﷻ revealed the following verse regarding their situation:

> *It may be if he divorced you [all] that his Lord will give him instead of you, wives better than you—Muslims [who submit to Allah], believers, obedient [to Allah], turning to Allah in repentance, worshipping Allah sincerely, given to fasting or emigrants [for Allah's sake], previously married and virgins. (Qur'an 66:5)*

Nowhere in this verse did Allah say that divorce is unacceptable.

There were also times when the Prophet ﷺ allowed immediate divorce, like in the case of Thabit ibn Qays's wife (may Allah be pleased with them both). As we learn in *Sahih al-Bukhari*, Ibn Abbas (may Allah be pleased with him) narrated that the wife of Thabit ibn Qays came to the Prophet ﷺ and said, "Oh Messenger of Allah, I do not blame Thabit ibn Qays for any defect in his character or his religious commitment, but I would hate to commit an act of disbelief now that I am a Muslim." The Prophet ﷺ asked her, "Will you give him back his garden [that he gave you as a dowry]?" She said, "Yes." The Prophet ﷺ said to Thabit, "Take your garden back and divorce her once." In another narration, Ibn Abbas said, "He commanded him to divorce her."

At other times, the Prophet suggested exploring reconciliation, as in the case of Barirah (may Allah be pleased with her). The following story was narrated from Ibn Abbas: "The husband of Barirah was a slave called Mughith (may Allah be pleased with him). It is as if I can see him walking behind her weeping, with the tears running down onto his beard. The Prophet ﷺ said to al-Abbas, "Oh Abbas, are you not amazed by the love of Mughith for Barirah and the hatred of Barirah for Mughith?" The Messenger of Allah said to her, "Why don't you take him back, for he is the father of your child?" She said, "Oh Messenger of Allah, are you commanding me [to do so]?" He said, "I am just interceding." She said, "I have no need of him" (*Sunan al-Nasa'i*).

This hadith is so beautiful and full of lessons. We see that her husband was very open about his feelings for her. We also see that she sought to clarify whether the Prophet ﷺ was ordering her to stay with Mughith. Whatever her reasons for not wanting to stay with her husband, she felt it necessary to walk away from him. The Prophet ﷺ did not admonish her for her decision, and he did not insist she stay with him either, despite his advice to reconsider.

There is no evidence in Islam to say that divorce is a sin or that Allah will punish you for it, regardless of your reasons. If divorce was inherently a bad and impermissible thing to do, the Prophet ﷺ wouldn't have allowed it.

It is important to have a sense of confidence that you did the best you could, given what you knew at the time. The hadith about Allah ﷻ hating divorce is not an invitation to continually question your decision postdivorce. It is normal to question the decision during the bargaining stage, while attempting to salvage the marriage. Once the divorce is final, many women continue to experience extreme guilt, fearing they have angered Allah despite having valid reasons to pursue their divorce.

Of course, a decision to divorce should not be taken lightly. It should be a deliberate, meticulous process undertaken while constantly asking Allah ﷻ for guidance. However, even if your divorce was due to a frivolous reason or if you consider it a mistake later, the appropriate response is not to dwell in guilt and repeatedly bring up this hadith. Allah ﷻ forgives even the most heinous crimes if there is genuine remorse and sincerity. Once the dust settles and you realize the divorce is done, don't use this hadith as a crutch to be stuck in perpetual guilt, crippling your ability to move on with life. Remember that you did not commit a sin—divorce is allowed in Islam! Make *tawba* (repentence) for your mistakes, and then focus on recognizing what the lessons of the divorce may be.

Facing the Stigma

In Nathaniel Hawthorne's classic novel, *The Scarlet Letter*, Hester Prynne has a child out of wedlock and is condemned to wear a scarlet *A* on her chest, marking her as an adulteress for life. This symbol of shame and public humiliation isolates her from society and serves as a constant reminder of her sin.

Although divorce is permissible in Islam, it is often surrounded by a cloud of stigma. Within some communities, individuals who undergo a divorce are ostracized as if they wear an invisible letter *D* for "divorcee." This mark can lead to a lifetime of judgment, gossip, and exclusion, making the already painful process of divorce even more challenging. Our community uses the label as though it is branded onto us, as if we are the embodiment of undesirability. However, divorce is not something that we are; it is simply a circumstance that we go through.

Many divorced women face scrutiny and blame, with society quick to judge without understanding the circumstances that led to the dissolution of the marriage. This stigma manifests itself in various forms: difficulty in finding new marital prospects, loss of friends, and even strained family relationships.

It's crucial for communities to create a supportive environment where divorcees can rebuild their lives without the burden of judgment. The invisible *D* should not be a mark of shame but rather an opportunity for offering support, empathy, and new beginnings. In some ways, our community seems to think that divorce is a sign of our collective failure, an indication that this person has betrayed the whole community.

Those facing divorce are already facing a time of loneliness, doubt, and anxiety during an arduous process that shakes their very foundation and sense of being. But instead of being there for them and providing them with support, we—our entire society— add fuel to the fire by shutting them out. Our cold attitudes and constant guilt-tripping won't save their marriages or help them embrace a better future, which is what we *should* ultimately want for them.

The Prophet 鬱 said to love for your brother what you love for yourself. Aren't compassion and love what we want for those going through something tough? Would we want criticism and stigma instead? The Prophet 鬱 also said the *ummah* (global community of Muslims) is like one body. Someone broken by divorce is still part of the bigger picture, part of the *ummah*. If someone is left to suffer in a state of brokenness, rest assured that this will have far-reaching consequences for the entire *ummah* in the long run.

However, stigma is not a one-way street. Often, the stigma comes from ourselves, too, because we are also coming from the same fabric of society that perpetuates these irrational beliefs.

If stigma, whether from yourself or others, feels present in your divorce, here are some practical ways to combat its negative effects:

1. Know that divorce was always in your *qadr*. Remember that this decision was the best thing for you, because Allah 鬱 chose it for you.

2. Change the story you are telling yourself. When we are ashamed and see ourselves as failures, we imagine that everyone is thinking that we are failures too. But we are all equally imperfect humans, with our own limiting beliefs and biased experiences. How someone views us is outside of our circle of influence; it is not within our control.

3. Choose to make your divorce the beginning of the rest of your life. Use this change as an opportunity to learn from and become a better person than you were before. If you can truly achieve this, your attitude will change, your energy

will change, and your whole life will change for the better. As the famous saying commonly attributed to Ali ibn Abu Talib goes, "The best revenge is to improve yourself."

4. Remember that the Day of Judgment is closer than we realize. In the grand scheme of things, we are only moments away from the only Day that really matters.

The day man will flee from his own brother, his mother, his father, his wife, his children. Each of them will be absorbed in concerns of their own on that day. (Qur'an 80:34–37)

Why should we be worried about people who will only be concerned with their own deeds? Inevitably, we will *all* only be concerned with our own deeds.

5. Remember that our purpose is not to seek approval from everyone else. Our goal is not to show them how great our life is. Rather, the only purpose we have in life is to please Allah ﷻ. If praise is to come from anyone, let it be from Allah ﷻ and the angels.

Allah ﷻ created a world that drives us to Him. Our visions, dreams, and roles may provide some identity and purpose, but they are all illusions. In the end, there is only Him. Our purpose in life is to submit to this reality. You, my sister, need a radical identity upgrade. It was this same upgrade that saved me from wallowing in guilt, shame, and self-pity and allowed me to step into my ultimate purpose. Are you ready?

CHALLENGE

Your challenge for this chapter is to examine and deal with your beliefs about divorce in Islam. This is the beginning of coming to terms with your divorce.

1. What beliefs do you hold about divorce?

2. How do these beliefs impact your perception of yourself and your future?

3. How can understanding that Allah dislikes divorce in general, but also wants well-being for you and permits divorce, help you find peace and release unnecessary guilt and shame?

4. What two methods will you use to combat stigma and judgment you may feel toward yourself?

3

The Self

I hung up the phone feeling worse than I had when I picked it up to call my friend. Talking to her about the divorce left me even more dejected; she didn't have any useful advice, just empty platitudes. I realized I needed someone impartial, so I reached out to a life coach I knew, an old schoolmate. The first few sessions were light and informal. A few weeks later, we finally broached the topic of my divorce. I found myself bristling after every session, although I nodded politely throughout.

There was one session where I was recounting some of the actions of my ex-husband that were upsetting. After I was finished with my long list of his crimes, I looked at her eagerly, expecting pity or some level of indignation on my behalf. Instead, her response was, "What if the way you see things is not reality? What if this is only your perception of reality?"

How dare she question me?

Wasn't it clear what a bad person my ex was?

Wasn't I the victim in all of this?

I felt like chucking the empty Starbucks cup nearby at her face on the screen, but my people-pleasing instinct kicked in and I responded positively.

She then asked a question that sparked a profound journey of self-discovery and forever changed my life.

She asked me to answer the question, "Who are you?" Initially, I found it straightforward. Confidently, I told her it didn't even need to be homework. I answered, portraying myself as a strong woman shaped by life's challenges and listing roles like being a mom, and I thought I had it covered. However, she redirected me, emphasizing that my roles weren't my true identity. She urged me to use a spiritual lens and reframed it as, "What does your religion teach you about who you are?" At that point, I felt a little lost. I told her I would think about it and come back with the answer the following week, as she had originally requested.

I took the assignment seriously and spent the week searching my soul for the right answer. All I could think of were the answers I had given her already, with one addition: "I am God's creation."

I even went online and searched "who am I Islam." I combed website after website, going down rabbit holes left, right, and center. When I showed up to the next session, I proudly presented my answer:

> *I am a spiritual being having a physical experience on earth.*
> *I am a spirit contained within a physical body, created for*
> *the ultimate purpose of worshipping Allah using a variety of*
> *means. My purpose in this dunya should ultimately serve my*

higher purpose, all while achieving satisfaction for my spirit
and servicing others during my stay in this physical realm.

My response seemed sophisticated but felt incomplete. I read it to her, but I wasn't connected to what I wrote. That same week, I found myself randomly picking up the book *Purification of the Heart*, by Shaykh Hamza Yusuf. It felt like Allah had decided to have a conversation with me at that moment.

Many in the West have long proffered that the brain is the center of consciousness. But in traditional Islamic thought—as in other traditions—the heart is viewed as the center of our being. The Qur'an, for example, speaks of wayward people who have hearts "with which they do not understand" (Qur'an 7:179). Also the Qur'an mentions people who mocked the Prophet ﷺ and were entirely insincere in listening to his message, so God "placed over their hearts a covering that they may not understand it and in their ears [He placed] acute deafness" (Qur'an 6:25). Their inability to understand is a deviation from the spiritual function of a sound heart, just as their ears have been afflicted with a spiritual "deafness." So we understand from this that the center of the intellect, the center of human consciousness and conscience, is actually the heart and not the brain. Only recently have we discovered that there are over 40,000 neurons in the heart. In other words, there are cells in the heart that are communicating with the brain. While the brain sends messages to the heart, the heart also sends messages to the brain.

I was astounded to learn about the heart's intelligence. My education had emphasized Darwinian theory, downplaying any spiritual or inner world. Deep down, humans seemed more a product of random evolution than sacred beings. Here I was, searching for answers about who I was, and a piece of the puzzle had fallen into my lap. Something big was about to open up in front of me, an indication that there was more to me and my essence than the terms I kept adopting and dodging to define my identity.

I took this development to my coach the following week, excited to share my findings with her. The divorce heartaches didn't come up even once; I was too engrossed with my new discovery.

"You know how there are expressions like 'he broke my heart,' and 'she wears her heart on her sleeve'? They're not just empty expressions!" I told her that, according to my faith, my heart has the ability to discern what is right or wrong. I don't only use my brain! This experience launched a search for deeper meaning that lasted for the better part of a year. I wanted to know more. What else was hiding within me?

I emailed two shaykhs, but only one responded politely, providing sparse information and not addressing my specific question. Disappointed, I explored Barnes & Noble. While I found a diverse range of books, many contained metaphysical concepts that contradicted my beliefs as a Muslim.

Despite our rich Islamic heritage and access to extensive knowledge, the information I needed was dishearteningly difficult to find. I did not know where or how to look for answers about what makes me a human and the internal dimensions I carried within me. I longed to know more about my rich inner world. I did not give up; week after week, I combed through bookstores in my city.

Who am I, really? Before this frenzied search, I'd never spent time thinking about this question before. Was there a chance that I was more than my divorce? Was it possible that I was more than just my job or my marital status?

It was not until I enrolled in a class about African Sufis that things became less hazy. I joined the class out of curiosity, interested in exploring an unfamiliar subject; I did not think it had anything to do with my search. However, Allah ﷻ had a treat in store for me.

The instructor, Dr. Bilal Ware, introduced us to the concept of the inner dimensions of the human being from the lens of the Qur'an and Sunnah. He discussed the soul, the ego, and the heart as a spiritual entity. I sat there, awestruck at how this information provided answers to so many of my questions.

I took another class, Dr. Marwa Assar's God and Me Program. Initially, I joined it to improve my spirituality and relationship with Allah ﷻ. Among the many gems of the program was a section on the internal dimensions of the human self. As with the African Sufis class, this course gave me the answers I was looking for, reinforcing and driving the lessons home even more. Even though I hadn't made any specific *du'a* (prayer), Allah answered my unspoken desire to know myself in every way. What I learned changed the way I looked at myself and the world around me forever.

In the following section, I'll share the basics of what I learned, which are essential and valuable for anyone on a journey of spiritual development and self-awareness. These lessons became the foundation of my new identity after divorce, and they can serve as yours too.

What Makes Up a Human?

As Imam Al-Ghazali said in his book *The Alchemy of Happiness*, "He who knows himself is truly happy." There is another famous saying from the early Muslims, "He who knows himself knows His Lord." Knowing ourselves starts with a basic understanding of what makes us up in the first place.

The combination of the apparent physical body and the following interior elements make up a human's holistic existence: the heart (*qalb*), the spirit (*ruh*), the soul (*nafs*), and the intelligence (*'aql*). In his renowned work *Ihya ulum al-din*, Imam Al-Ghazali goes through each of these terms and explains the dual meanings of each concept.

The Heart (Qalb)

The heart, while physically responsible for pumping blood, also embodies a profound spiritual dimension. The heart is the innermost consciousness, the essence of a human. In the Qur'an, it is mentioned about 137 times. The heart is where revelation descends, as this verse shows us:

> *Whoever is an enemy of Gabriel should know that he revealed this [Qur'an] to your heart by Allah's Will. (Qur'an 2:97)*

This verse highlights the heart as the seat of divine knowledge. When the heart, as the leader, is in a state of spiritual goodness, that goodness flows into everything we do. Imam Al-Ghazali describes the heart as "a subtle, tenuous substance . . . the real essence of man."

Modern science has begun exploring the idea of the heart's intelligence. Researcher Howard Martin and the HeartMath organization have shown that heart rhythms shift with emotional states—erratic when frustrated, smooth when appreciative. This research is beginning to prove that the heart is far more than just a blood-pumping organ, resonating with Islam's teachings.

In Western culture, however, the spiritual heart is often overlooked. George Makari, in *Soul Machine: The Invention of the Modern Mind*, examines how, during the seventeenth and eighteenth centuries, shifting religious and scientific perspectives led to the replacement of the concept of the immortal soul with the modern understanding of the mind.

The Spirit (Ruh)

In the Qur'an, the term *ruh* is used to signify something that brings life, help, or guidance. It is mentioned in connection with the angel Jibreel, who delivered revelations to the prophets (16:102 and 26:193). The Qur'an itself is also referred to as *ruh* because it brings life and guidance to humanity (42:52). Additionally, *ruh* is mentioned in reference to Isa (peace be upon him) (4:171 and 21:91).

Regarding human creation, the Qur'an describes *ruh* as a life force "blown" into beings (15:29 and 32:9). In the Sunnah, the *ruh* is referenced in ahadith, such as when it is breathed into a mother's womb to animate the fetus. The Prophet ﷺ also told us that the eyes follow the *ruh* as it exits the body at death. Despite these insights, the *ruh* remains a mystery. Allah says, "[Prophet], they ask you about the spirit [*ruh*]. Say, 'The spirit is part of my Lord's domain. You have only been given a little knowledge'" (Qur'an

17:85). Imam Al-Ghazali describes the *ruh* as "a wondrous, heavenly matter" that eludes full human comprehension, highlighting its ineffable nature.

The Soul (Nafs)

The *nafs* represents our base self, which is tied to desires and survival instincts but is also capable of refinement and purity. The *nafs* is essential for ensuring our survival needs are met, and when balanced, it can reach a state known as "the soul at peace," as described in the Qur'an: "[But] you, soul at peace: return to your Lord well pleased and well pleasing" (Qur'an 89:27–28).

Imam Al-Ghazali explains that the *nafs* has layers of meaning. At its base, he identifies it with anger and desire. However, he also describes it as the essence of a human being:

> *The second meaning is that subtle, tenuous substance we mentioned, which is, in reality, man. It is the soul of man and his essence. But it is described by different terms according to its varying states. When it is at peace under His command, and agitation has left it on account of its opposition to the fleshly appetites, it is called "the soul at rest"* [al-nafs al-mutma'inna].

This layered understanding of *nafs* reveals it as both the base self and the highest, tranquil state achievable through spiritual discipline.

Intelligence ('Aql)

The term *'aql* is usually translated as "intelligence," referring to the conscious awareness that enables humans to understand, learn, and exercise self-restraint. Imam Al-Ghazali describes it as the power that allows humans to perceive, recognize, and moderate their behavior. He further defines it as the ability to perceive and know, similar to the function of the heart.

In Islamic thought, *'aql* is an expansive concept distinct from the conventional Western ideas of the brain or mind. It serves as a moral compass, encouraging believers to reflect, seek knowledge, and make decisions aligned with divine principles. It also implies restraint, providing a means for individuals to manage desires and avoid poor choices. This brings to mind (pun intended) the common phrase, "Have you lost your mind?"—a phrase often used when someone acts foolishly, suggesting a loss of control or a failure of reason.

————

The topic of our inner life is complex and could easily occupy a lifetime of exploration. It is a topic that has interested people and been discussed even before Islam. It is certainly not something I have extensive knowledge of, as evident from my brief descriptions in this book. And the ultimate truth is known only by Allah ﷻ. I hope, however, that this material has been sufficient to demonstrate that the human being is an extraordinary, intricate, and awe-inspiring creation of Allah ﷻ—a profound sign of His majesty and boundless power. Just look at the inner realities we carry: the depth, complexity, and mystery within us, each aspect a reflection of Allah's limitless knowledge and grandeur.

————

Within the span of a year of learning about the rich spiritual traditions of Islam, I became convinced that I am so much more than a physical collection of cells with the ability to walk upright. I became a spiritual being with meaning and purpose.

Sure, I had always considered myself a Muslim: I prayed, fasted, and believed in Judgment Day and that I would be questioned for my wrongdoings and ultimately placed in either the eternal bliss of Jannah or the unending torment of Jahannam. It was a simplistic understanding of life and the afterlife. But a revelation danced at the edge of my consciousness, just out of reach. After mulling over my discoveries, it dawned on me—I was not my divorce after all! And neither are you!

1. We are much more than a clump of cells. We have an everlasting inner world, one that has transcendent value.
2. We have a purpose that is bigger than our circumstances or day-to-day struggles.
3. Our circumstances in life don't define who we are; we are not "just divorcees."
4. Our worth is not tied to our circumstances. We are valuable because of who we are and who chose to bring us forth—Allah ﷻ.
5. Every single person on this planet is being tested in different ways. Divorce is a particularly difficult test simply because humans have attached marriage to what makes a woman whole.

You and I are so much bigger than our struggles. We are more complicated, complex, and amazing than we could ever fathom. When we understand our internal realities and our purpose, we will navigate life differently.

Defined by Circumstance

A lot of us define ourselves by the circumstances we find ourselves in. Consider the following: A woman from a middle-class family, raised with all her needs met, excels academically and secures a well-paying job, meeting her family's high expectations of success. She works hard and enjoys the perks of her successful career. However, after making a critical mistake at work, she is fired and unable to find another job in her field, forcing her to take a minimum-wage job at McDonald's. How do you think this woman feels? If she has tied her identity to being a successful woman with money, a good job, and property, she will likely feel a sense of shame and embarrassment at having "failed." She may experience a loss of identity and direction. However, if she understands that she is *not* defined by her job, then the way she perceives herself will be different, despite the hardships.

Whether you are born in the slums of a developing country, lose your husband, and end up alone with five kids or are never married and spend your entire life studying penguins in the North Pole, none of these things are **who** you are. They are merely the circumstances of your life.

At the end of the day, you are a creation of Allah ﷻ, with both an internal dimension and a physical experience in this world. Allah sent you here temporarily for a mission; this is not even your permanent home. You are a guest. When you divorce yourself (pun intended) from the divorce (or whatever circumstance is currently holding you back), when you stop equating it with your identity, you will value yourself more. It will be easier to handle life's challenges because they won't define who you are.

In our community, a lot of our headaches stem from internalizing and weaving the divorce into our very core, making it **who we are.** We need to learn to see it as just one chapter in our lives and do our best to make sure the trials we face are met with excellence. At the end of the day, we just want to fulfill our purpose and go to our permanent home—Jannah. So what is our purpose? That is what we will explore in detail in the next chapter.

CHALLENGE

Your challenge for this chapter is to sincerely and truly reflect on who you are—your entire self, with all its complexity and depth. This reflection is meant to help you move beyond the immediate emotions of divorce and into a deep exploration of your identity as a human being.

1. Reflect on each part of your inner self. Who are you beyond the social roles you play (e.g., wife, mother, professional)?

2. What are some ways you can honor and reconnect with the full depth of who you are beyond your marital status?

3. How can having a deeper understanding of yourself push you to see beyond the label of a "divorcee" and recognize your true value and importance in the world?

4. How can you view divorce as a temporary challenge rather than a permanent setback?

4

Fulfilling Your Ultimate Purpose

My mother once brought home a curious cylindrical object from a thrift store. After days of puzzlement and a series of hilarious mistaken guesses, we finally discovered that it was a dog feeder. Despite its intriguing design and low cost, she returned it, since we didn't have a dog. This incident always reminds me of a simple truth: Every man-made product exists to fulfill a specific function, much like each of us in this world.

Many people walk around in a daze because they don't have a sense of purpose. As Muslims, we are truly blessed because Allah ﷻ has given us clear guidance on life's purpose and how to live it fully. Just like the items we use on a daily basis; we too have a purpose. We need to fulfill it, and only by fulfilling this purpose will we find balance.

Animals fulfill their purpose purely by instinct. A mother octopus fiercely defends her eggs, choosing to starve rather than abandon her post. Dogs guard diligently, even in the absence of livestock. Migrating birds stay on course despite countless distractions, driven by an instinctive sense of purpose. Their focus is so sharp that they pass by food they would normally stop for under usual circumstances.

If all this is true of animals, what of us humans? What is our purpose? Allah ﷻ tells us in the Qur'an, "And I [Allah] created not the jinn and humankind except that they should worship Me [alone]" (Qur'an 51:56).

This verse provides us with a direct and unequivocal answer: Our purpose is to worship Allah. Since we have a transcendent purpose and are under Allah's sovereignty, our purpose is about aligning our actions, decisions, and life choices with what is pleasing to Allah. Just as an ambassador acts only in accordance with their country's government's rules, we too must act within the boundaries of Allah and fulfill what we were sent here for. This verse shows us the basis of our purpose; it is the foundation. But our purpose goes beyond that, and we'll explore it further.

Here are a few ways to ensure your whole life is worship: Make intentions for everything you do and embrace gratitude and/or patience in all of the circumstances of your life.

The Prophet ﷺ told us that actions are judged in accordance with intentions, and that everyone will be rewarded based on intentions. In fulfilling our purpose of knowing and worshipping Allah, everything we do, from the mundane to the significant, can be intended for the sake of Allah. Umar ibn al-Khattab (may Allah be pleased with him) reported: The Messenger of Allah ﷺ said,

"Verily, deeds are only by intentions, and every person will have only what they intended" (*Sahih al-Bukhari* and *Sahih Muslim*).

We can transform any task from meaning*less* to meaning*ful* through the power of our intentions. Even something as necessary as sleep can be a form of worship by setting the intention that you are doing it to fulfill the *amanah* (the trust) of nurturing the body Allah has given you.

In life, everything that happens can either evoke our gratitude or patience. The Prophet ﷺ told us: "How wondrous is the affair of the believer! There is good for them in every matter, and this is not the case with anyone except the believer. If they are happy, then they thank Allah and thus there is good for them, and if they are harmed, then they show patience and thus there is good for them" (*Sahih Muslim*).

If every situation we face elicits either patience or gratitude, it becomes a form of worship, and therefore rewardable.

Humanity's Purpose as a Whole

If aligning our actions with what makes Allah happy is the basic level of fulfilling our purpose of worship, what does the bigger picture of purpose look like?

Allah ﷻ told us in Surat al-Baqara that we are the authority and the leader—the *khalifa*—on Earth.

> [Prophet], when your Lord told the angels, "I am putting a
> successor on earth," they said, "How can You put someone
> there who will cause damage and bloodshed, when we
> celebrate Your praise and proclaim Your holiness?" but
> He said, "I know things you do not." (Qur'an 2:30)

This verse always makes me feel special. Allah knows something about us, which the angels are not privy to, that made Him put *us* on Earth as an authority! Allah presented the trust of this leadership, and only we rose to the occasion. It is an *amanah* to choose to obey Allah ﷻ.

As a *khalifa*, we are meant to serve others as a way of fulfilling this trust. Every single one of us came into this world as stewards of Allah's creation, and we are entrusted with embodying the role. The title *khalifa* holds profound significance—it calls us to a purpose beyond mere existence. Realizing this trust means embracing our potential and contributing meaningfully to the world.

The ways we fulfill this duty are unique to each of us, shaped by the inclinations Allah has gifted us with. Perhaps you're a skilled herbalist with the gift of healing, a writer with a way with words, or someone who excels with children, called to teach the next generation. What is your "genius zone"?

Though the responsibility of *khilafa* (stewardship) is shared, each individual's efforts are vital to the well-being and success of the whole. We will explore this concept further in Chapter 5: Self-Worth.

Life's Purpose in the Context of Divorce

If our purpose is to know and worship Allah, face tests, and reach our full potential by serving others, what role does our divorce have in this journey?

Everything we go through in this *dunya* (worldly life) can be a way to come closer to Allah ﷻ. Divorce is no different. If even going to sleep can be a form of worship, what about divorce? No matter how painful the divorce, what will it draw out of us? Will it help us grow closer to our Creator?

It was the will of Allah ﷻ that we would experience divorce. We need to pause and consider how we will let this experience impact us: for better or for worse? Handling the test of divorce with grace, conscientiousness, and reliance on Allah ﷻ is a beautiful way to worship Him. Do we react with *tawakkul* (trust) in and patience with Allah's plans? Do we attempt to extract the spiritual and emotional lessons of this experience? Will we choose to honor this journey in a way that will make Allah ﷻ pleased with us?

If we stumble on an opportunity to hurt our former husband, for example, in a court of law, will we choose to exercise *taqwa* (mindfulness of Allah) and be truthful?

If our angry family encourages negative actions, will we choose to obey Allah ﷻ instead and exercise control?

If we feel tempted to withhold access to the children, will we choose to rise above that feeling and be just?

What Can Divorce with Purpose Look Like?

Divorce with purpose means to actively choose to behave with *taqwa* of Allah no matter the situation. It involves resisting all harmful behaviors, whether it's the temptation to seek revenge or withhold access to the children, or to simply refrain from sharing every negative sentiment about your ex with anyone who will listen. **At the most basic level, worshipping Allah means staying within the boundaries Allah set for us.** When it comes to divorce, here is what that can look like:

1. Separate the divorce from the destination

Our ultimate destination, the finish line of our very existence, is our meeting with Allah ﷻ. Every journey we face has the potential to guide us there while benefiting us. Divorce is not the end of the world. Don't let yourself fall into the trap of believing that your divorce is your final destination, because there is so much more yet to come.

2. Control your actions

It is extremely difficult at times, but we must always remember to act in a way that does not incur Allah's anger. No matter how furious you are or how much emotional pain you are in, adhere to what is pleasing to Allah. Allah says:

> *Oh you who believe! Stand out firmly for Allah as just witnesses; and let not **the enmity and hatred of others make you avoid justice. Be just**: that is nearer to piety; and fear Allah. Verily, Allah is Well-Acquainted with what you do. (Qur'an 5:8)*

Allah ﷻ is teaching us not to allow animosity to cloud our sense of justice.

3. Purify your intentions

Remember the importance of *niyyah* (intention) and how it can transform the mundane into the spiritual. You can turn the daily struggles and pains of divorce into acts of worship by setting positive intentions. In moments of despair or when dealing with difficult situations, intentionally ask Allah ﷻ to accept these challenges as acts of worship.

All the pain and heartache we go through can be a way to amass rewards. Even while hurting, set the intention that is most beneficial to you—worship. Why suffer in vain when you can turn it into gold, simply by asking Allah ﷻ to be pleased with your patience and accept it from you?

4. Cultivate patience and trust in Allah ﷻ

Everything can be a path to Allah ﷻ, including divorce. Getting a job or losing one, accepting a proposal or canceling a wedding, having children or being infertile . . . All of these situations are tests and can either be a path to Allah or a path away from Him. What matters is your perspective and how you choose to react to these tests. Will you turn to Allah, trust in Him, and become more reliant on Him?

Divorce and Duty as a *Khalifa*

At a higher level of our purpose to serve Allah's creation, divorce can play a significant role. You can use your experience to support other women in your local masjid who are going through similar situations. You might even create something larger, like a nonprofit organization that could grow into a worldwide initiative over the years. You could write a book about your journey. Alternatively, you might choose a different path altogether, where the lessons you learned help you fulfill another divine purpose you feel called to. Even though we understand all the concepts discussed above, sometimes our own self-perceptions can be so clouded and skewed that it may be hard to internalize these beliefs. In the next section, we will explore self-worth to help us embrace our purpose and ourselves more fully.

CHALLENGE

Your challenge in this chapter is to upgrade your understanding of purpose and divine duty. You are to look beyond your divorce and align with a higher calling—your purpose in life as a believer.

1. Reflect on purpose: What has been your understanding of purpose so far?

2. Choose three activities or challenges that feel routine or burdensome. How could you transform each into an act of worship?

3. One of your roles is to be a *khalifa*—a steward and leader. What are your thoughts on this divine duty, and how might seeing yourself as a *khalifa* influence your daily choices?

4. Imagine your life with your actions, career, and relationships fully aligned with your higher purpose as a *khalifa* on Earth. What would this look like? Try to be as detailed as possible when visualizing.

5. In the context of divorce, what could "fulfilling your purpose" look like? Think about areas such as personal growth or guiding your children.

5

Self-Worth

A few days before my *nikah* (marriage), I asked my ex-husband, "What would you do if I called off the *nikah*?" I played it off as a joke, but the truth was that I was desperate for validation.

Before I got married, I looked forward to marriage giving me a feeling of enoughness, of approval, of worth. I had expected my husband to be my knight in shining armor whose love would last forever. Getting divorced made me feel like a less-than-desirable part of society. I felt somehow dirty and tainted—a discarded *fet*. In fact, even worse than a *fet*. As undesirable as being a *fet* was, it didn't feel right to claim even *that*. The particular circumstances of my marriage—not having lived with my ex and not even making it to a year—made me feel like maybe my marriage wasn't even significant enough for me to "earn" the title of *fet*. In my mind, I was suspended in a weird limbo. I was undefined.

After a lot of introspection, I came to realize the truth: My struggle with self-worth had been there all along. The divorce just brought it to the surface. This is one example of the ways divorce can be a beautiful gift—an awakening to your inner world and a profound exploration of your true self, warts and all.

What Do You Base Your Worth On?

When I was growing up, my mother sent us to one of the best schools in Ethiopia even though she could barely afford it. School was not just "school"; it was a predictor of our future success. The emphasis on good grades was fierce; anything less than near perfect was unacceptable.

As a result, I learned to base my worth on my achievements. High grades would result in my mother's happiness; anything less would mean her disappointment, which would make me feel small. As an adult, even though I did not realize it, this was a standard I kept holding myself to even after school. It changed forms, but there was always something that I needed to be good at so that I could, in turn, feel good about myself. I did not find value in myself unless others approved of me or unless I accomplished something new.

Many of us have learned to base our value on our beauty, careers, possessions, marital status, role as a parent, relationships, and so on. In short, we place our value on external factors that we have little control over. But in the absence of those things, are we now valueless? If you are not married until you turn fifty, is your identity that of a woman who couldn't manage to find a husband until middle age? If you get divorced and are now responsible for four kids under ten, is your identity that of a divorced single mom, struggling to stay afloat? If you are unable to have children, is your identity the barren one? These are situations in your life. You are not those labels. Your self-worth comes from *who you are, from simply being Allah's creation*. It also comes from your purpose in life and your individual qualities and character as a person. We naturally seek support and validation from others, but over time, we must learn to define our worth from within. Relying too much on external validation leaves us vulnerable and unable to stand firm when others aren't there to "hold" us emotionally.

Basing our opinion of ourselves on what other people think of us, whether family, society, or spouse, is not healthy or helpful. What if your family or spouse does not see you as worthy? Are you now going to believe that you are inherently worthless? Is your idea of yourself going to fluctuate based on how others view you? Remember, you are not responsible for others' actions or how they think. Seeking validation from others may be natural and can be beneficial for building relationships, but it also has the potential to lead to a slippery slope of disappointment. Our core sense of worth and ultimate validation should come from Allah ﷻ.

Generating Self-Worth

Self-worth is the respect and value you have for yourself and a sense of peace with who you are, imperfections and all. Self-worth is the belief that you are enough as a person; it is the ability to accept your imperfections without constantly striving for unattainable ideals or external validation. However, self-worth isn't something you either have or don't have. It's not a simple yes or no. Self-worth is a vision of yourself in your mind, so it fluctuates based on what may be going on in your life. The goal is to maintain a strong sense of self-worth on most days, and, during tough times, to have the tools to guide you out of the darkness. There are three cornerstones of self-worth, and they collectively make up a strong sense of self. If we have worth in just one or two, then it may feel like there is something missing.

Self-worth can be divided into three categories:

1. **Innate Self-Worth.** Intrinsic worth comes from within; it is a gift Allah has given us simply because He created us as humans. This worth is unlocked by understanding who we are, why we are here, and where we are going, which gives us purpose and direction.
2. **Self-Worth Based on Service.** A sense of worthiness comes from caring for and helping others. Service is about adding value to the world.
3. **Self-Worth Based on Effort.** Taking action toward the worthy things we want provides a sense of worth. This is about making the effort to bring either the character traits or life goals we want into fruition.

Let's examine each of these categories more deeply.

Innate Self-Worth

Being human inherently carries dignity solely because we are creations of Allah ﷻ. If you find yourself grappling with self-loathing despite this divine honor, you may be failing to recognize the innate worth bestowed upon you. The sense of rejection that accompanies divorce can further shake this foundation of self-worth.

Allah ﷻ chose us to be born, to play a specific role while we live on this earth, and to eventually go to Jannah, inshallah. Allah ﷻ created you, made nature available to you for your provision, gave you a heart with intelligence, and sent the Qur'an to tell you what the plan is . . . And you dare to think that you are not important?

Verses in the Qur'an reveal how Allah honored us with dignity and careful design:

> *And He has subjected to you the night and the*
> *day, and the sun and the moon; and the stars are*
> *subjected by His Command. Surely, in this are proofs*
> *for people who understand. (Qur'an 16:12)*

> *He has subjected all that is in the heavens and the earth*
> *for your benefit, as a gift from Him. There truly are*
> *signs in this for those who reflect. (Qur'an 45:13)*

> *We have honored the children of Adam and carried*
> *them by land and sea; We have provided good*
> *sustenance for them and favored them specially above*
> *many of those We have created. (Qur'an 17:70)*

Allah ﷻ clearly told us of the high honor and dignity He has bestowed upon us in more than one place; that by itself is an indication of our worth. Think about it: Allah designed this world and placed us in it, equipping us with all we need to fulfill our purpose. The sun, moon, and stars aren't just cosmic details; they are reminders of our immense value. Being chosen as His honored creation means each of us holds unique worth. Feeling insignificant contradicts the truth Allah has set forth.

During ejaculation, millions of sperm cells race toward the egg, but only one succeeds in fertilizing it. Although any of the other sperm cells could have accomplished this, it was the sperm cell that led to *your* conception that was destined to fertilize it, leading to *you*. Another way to think about this is to imagine how many souls Allah ﷻ created in the unseen realm? He could have sent any one of them to your mother's womb, yet *you* were the soul specifically assigned to *your* mother and given a specific destiny of your own.

The believer is priceless to Allah ﷻ. It is not your circumstances, your appearance, or your wealth that Allah looks at. The Prophet ﷺ said, "Verily, Allah does not look at your appearance or wealth, but rather He looks at your hearts and actions" (*Sahih Muslim*). It is your status as a believer and your dedication to Him that matters to Allah.

Simply by virtue of Allah ﷻ choosing to create *you*, you are worthy. You don't need anything else to validate your worth. In Surat al-Baqara, Allah tells us that after He created Adam (peace be upon him), He told the angels to bow down to this new human creation. However, Shaytan refused to bow because he felt he was a superior creation to this being made of earthly clay. This story is usually told in the context of jealousy, arrogance, and disobedience to Allah. But have you ever thought about how special human beings are, and how Allah ﷻ honored us above the rest of creation, so much so that he commanded angels to bow down to us?

Your value as a woman exists far beyond the bounds of marriage or divorce. It comes from the undeniable truth that Allah ﷻ chose to bring you into this world—a deliberate act of creation that speaks to your inherent worth. You are not defined by your relationship status but by the unique inner qualities that make you, you. Your dignity, purpose, and worth remain untouched by the ending of a marriage, because your worth was never tied to it to begin with. You are, and always have been, valuable simply because you exist.

The next time you feel negative about yourself and question your worth, be as compassionate with yourself as you are with others, and gently remind yourself of the truth. Train yourself to become aware of negative perceptions and replace them. By consistently practicing this mental shift, you can cultivate a more positive and empowering perception of yourself. Do this as often and as long as necessary to see the transformation.

Ask Yourself . . .

What are your most dominant thoughts about yourself that are not helpful? List as many as you can. Then, replace them with something positive. The next time one of the old, negative thoughts surfaces, replace it with the positive one. This is an exercise you will have to do on an ongoing basis. The more you do it, the faster you will get at catching and replacing.

Examples

Old thought: "I'll never find happiness again after my divorce."

New thought: "This divorce is a difficult experience, but it opens the door to new possibilities and happiness that I might not have discovered otherwise."

Old thought: "I failed at marriage, so I must be a failure in life."

New thought: "A divorce is an experience I can learn from, and it doesn't define my worth or my future success."

Old thought: "I am not pretty enough."

New thought: "Allah created me with beauty and purpose. My true value comes from the inner qualities that Allah has bestowed upon me, and I am beautiful just as I am."

Ask Yourself . . .

What are some things that help you remember that you have innate worth? What reminds you that Allah specifically chose to create *you*?

Self-Worth Based on Service

This category of self-worth comes from being of service to others, caring for others, giving compassion and love, and simply doing things for other people. Being in service to others allows us to both show and receive love and develop meaningful connections. Service allows you to be of value to society. It can be as simple as someone knowing their strengths and using them for the benefit of others while having a higher intention. It doesn't have to be something grandiose that makes you a household name.

Acts of service, whether small or large, are ways we add value to society. Islam teaches that the true worth of service lies not in recognition or fame but in fulfilling a higher purpose: serving others solely for the sake of Allah ﷻ. This hadith from the Prophet Muhammad ﷺ clearly shows how much Allah values those who bring benefit to others, along with the immense reward that such actions hold in both this life and the hereafter. The Prophet ﷺ said,

> The most beloved people to Allah are those who are most beneficial to people. The most beloved deed to Allah is to make a Muslim happy, or to remove one of his troubles, or to forgive his debt, or to feed his hunger. That I walk with a brother regarding a need is more beloved to me than that I seclude myself in this mosque in Medina for a month. . . . Whoever walks with his brother regarding a need until he secures it for him, then Allah Almighty will make his footing firm across the bridge on the day when the footings are shaken. (al-Tabarani)

There are various ways to benefit Allah's creation, and one of the simplest is by taking care of your family. Demonstrating love and kindness as a mother, daughter, friend, or neighbor and graciously receiving the love and support others offer can bring deep fulfillment. This may sound simple and straightforward, but cultivating genuine love in these various roles requires intentional effort and ongoing dedication. The act of loving nurtures your own self-worth and fulfillment, in addition to having a positive effect on the people who receive it.

Another form of being in service to others is using your talents and inclinations. Whatever your unique skills are, cultivate them and use them to benefit others. As we discussed above, Allah ﷻ loves those who benefit others. Using the gifts Allah ﷻ gave you is a form of showing gratitude for them. You will also grow in confidence as you see that you are a positive presence in others' lives, as long as you remember that everything good comes from Allah. Recognizing the source of our gifts keeps us appropriately humble.

Busying yourself with service to others will also provide you with a new focus, indirectly helping you cope with the divorce. A shift in your focus will make the emotions easier to deal with because the redirection of your energy helps cultivate a sense of purpose. You will be able to develop new skills while reinforcing your self-worth. Engaging with others in meaningful ways will also remind you that you're not alone in your struggles. It will also offer fresh insights that can make navigating your own challenges feel more manageable.

Below, you will find some questions to help you narrow down what your acts of service may be. You can fill in the answers in your workbook at www.makedayasenlul.com/divorcebookresources.

Figuring out your service

- What are you skilled at? Don't overthink it; it can be a skill you learned for work or even a hobby.

- Ask close friends or family: What do you think my strengths are? How do you think I could best help others?

- What inner battles or personal growth have shaped who you are today?

- When you reflect on your biggest triumphs and failures, what common threads do you see? How do they relate to your unique strengths and abilities?

- When you were a kid, what did you enjoy?

- What do you enjoy doing now?

- What talent feels underutilized in your life?

- What do you naturally do for others, sometimes without reward or recognition?

- What skill or knowledge do you have that feels effortless?

- What issue, problem, or area of need stirs something in you, making you feel called on to contribute a solution?

- What message or insight do you feel compelled to share with the world?

- If fear, doubt, or resources weren't an issue, what mission would you pursue for the rest of your life?

- Imagine you are observing your own funeral, and someone is speaking about your contribution, what do you want them to say? What legacy would you be disappointed to leave unfulfilled?

- Think of a time when you felt most alive or connected to something greater—what were you doing, and why did it resonate so deeply?

- Look at everything you have written above; do you notice a pattern? What do you feel most drawn to?

- How can you turn this thing you feel most drawn to into something beneficial for others? What angle of it feels like it can benefit others?

- What are some ways you can start taking action toward the choice you identified above? This can be part of a bigger goal that you've set for yourself and can be as big or small as you want. You might teach or simply share your art. For example, if you love writing, and had a life-changing experience, you can benefit others by sharing what you learned from the experience. For now, you can start by journaling or sharing your writing on social media. Or you can get started on a book! The action you take can be as big or small as you want, but start!

Self-Worth Based on Effort

The final category of self-worth includes the effort we put in to earn the things we want. This includes taking action toward the things we want to contribute to, the character we want to develop, or the relationships we want to maintain. There is a certain sense of healthy pride, joy, and self-respect that comes from making the effort to live a worthy life. But remember, the outcome of the effort is in Allah's hands; you are only in control of putting in the effort!

Effort is valuable in and of itself. Allah ﷻ sees and rewards our efforts, as the following verse tells us:

> And that each person will only have what they
> endeavored toward, and that the outcome of their
> endeavors will be seen in their record, then they
> will be fully rewarded. (Qur'an 53:39–41)

This verse teaches us that our efforts are valued not only by their outcomes but by the sincerity and dedication we invest in them. We will be fully rewarded based on our intentions and efforts. Ultimately, it's the genuine striving that matters most in the sight of Allah ﷻ, not merely the visible results. Every step taken in the right direction, regardless of the outcome, is seen and valued by Allah ﷻ.

Cultivating good habits. One way to get the most impact from your efforts is to establish good habits. Once a habit is in place, it becomes easier to do consistently, bringing greater reward from Allah ﷻ. The Prophet ﷺ said, "The most beloved deed to Allah is the most regular and constant, even if it is little" (*Sahih al-Bukhari*).

By turning your efforts into habits, you can maximize the benefits of your hard work. There are numerous resources available about building and maintaining habits, but here is my favorite simple yet powerful tip: Prepare your environment ahead of time. If you want to go for a walk tomorrow, lay out your exercise clothes and shoes by the door. To read more Qur'an, place your *mushaf* (copy of the Arabic Qur'an) where you often sit or beside your prayer rug. If you're aiming to restart writing, keep your journal and pen on your desk, ready to use. For intangible character goals, dedicate one day per week to embodying a specific trait, such as having a "Patience Day" where you consciously practice patience in all situations.

Earning Allah's love. One of the best ways to generate self-worth from effort is to align yourself with things that bring you closer to Allah ﷻ and earn His love. Earning Allah's love is deeply connected to self-worth because His love is what matters most.

"How do I know if Allah really loves me?" we may often ask ourselves, but the answer is simple. Allah has told us the actions and qualities that earn His love, providing a clear path to follow. This divine love reinforces our sense of worth, grounding it in the most profound and meaningful relationship we can have.

There are a plethora of teachings in our *deen* that show us how to earn the love of Allah ﷻ. Look into those and pick the ones you can do on a consistent basis. Integrate practices that bring you closer to Allah ﷻ into your daily routine.

Here are a few actions and qualities that earn us Allah's love:

1. Recite the Qur'an aloud

Make time to recite the Qur'an daily, even if only for a few minutes. The Qur'an is one of the main ways that we can build a relationship with Allah ﷻ.

Uthman ibn Affan (may Allah be pleased with him) reported: The Prophet ﷺ said, "The best of you are those who learn the Qur'an and teach it" (*Sahih al-Bukhari*).

Aisha (may Allah be pleased with her) reported: The Prophet ﷺ said, "Verily the one who recites the Qur'an beautifully, smoothly, and precisely, he will be in the company of the noble and obedient angels. And as for the one who recites with difficulty, stammering or stumbling through its verses, then he will have *twice* that reward" (*Sahih al-Bukhari*).

These ahadith show us the prestigious position the Qur'an can afford us if we make the effort to be close to it. The Qur'an is also described as *shifa* (healing) in various verses—for both physical and emotional healing. Now more than ever, it is important to start or improve our relationship with the Qur'an. What better way to start mending our broken hearts while earning Allah's love?

2. Make *dhikr*

Dhikr is the active practice of remembering Allah ﷻ. It is one avenue of earning Allah's love.

Numerous teachings in our *deen* emphasize the elevated status and immense rewards associated with consistently engaging in the remembrance of Allah. Here is one:

> *Whoever recites "La ilaha illa Allahu wahdahu la sharika lahu, lahul mulku wa lahul hamdu wa huwa 'ala kulli shay'in qadir" one hundred times in the day will receive the reward of freeing ten slaves, one hundred rewards will be written for him and one hundred sins wiped away, and he will be protected from Shaytan for the remainder of the day." (Sahih al-Bukhari)*

By incorporating *dhikr* into your daily routines, you don't just earn Allah's love, you cultivate inner peace. You feel fulfilled. You are reminded of His constant presence and mercy.

3. Pray 'Asr and Fajr on time

The Prophet ﷺ said,

> *Angels come to you in succession by night and day and all of them get together at the time of the Fajr and 'Asr prayers. Those who have passed the night with you [or stayed with you] ascend [to Heaven] and Allah asks them, though He knows everything about you, "In what state did you leave my slaves?" The angels reply: "When we left them, they were praying and when we reached them, they were praying." (Sahih al-Bukhari)*

As the hadith mentions, the angels change shifts at the time of 'Asr and Fajr. The ones who left us at 'Asr, if they left us praying, will come back at Fajr time, and, if they find us praying again, will mention this to Allah! Imagine being a permanent member of this blessed group! Knowing that you frequently do something that makes you mentioned by the angels and Allah gives you a special sense of honor and worth. If we do these good deeds consistently, aware of Allah's reward, imagine how much our own sense of value will increase!

4. Incorporate voluntary religious practices

What act of worship comes easily to you? Is it fasting? Performing extra prayers? Do you love to give *sadaqah* (charity) often? Abu Hurairah (may Allah be pleased with him) reported that the Messenger of Allah 🕌 said: "And My servant continues to draw near to me with *nafl* [extra] deeds until I love him" (*Sahih al-Bukhari*). Some small extra act of worship, done consistently, earns Allah's love. Find the act of worship that comes easiest to you and make it a regular part of your life. In doing so, you're creating a path that draws you closer to Allah and strengthens your bond with Him.

I must warn you, though, that the goal is to correct your own self-image and earn Allah's love. Be careful not to go to extremes and develop a sense of superiority over others. If you find yourself feeling this way, ask for Allah's forgiveness and get back on track. Life is a constant struggle of push and pull with various parts of ourselves. As long as you remain self-aware, you can correct course.

On the other hand, sometimes, we may feel frozen in survival mode due to all the emotional challenges of divorce, making even obligatory acts of worship, especially prayer, difficult to fulfill. If this is the state you're in now, remember that your prayer is valuable regardless of your emotions. Even if you don't feel it at the moment, you will still gain reward from Allah for the deed, simply because it is an obligation you are consistent in fulfilling. Despite the emotional overwhelm and the pain of your divorce, you are still prioritizing your obedience to Allah.

Ask Yourself . . .

What are some goals you want to make an effort toward? Which areas of personal growth feel most important to focus on right now?

What one habit, if established, would make achieving your goals easier? What small, consistent action could bring you closer to your goals of service?

Consider what earns Allah's love. What is one thing you can do consistently to earn it?

Mistakes and Self-Worth

When we sin or do something we are not proud of, we tend to devalue ourselves and think that we are irredeemable. However, even when we sin, Allah ﷻ does not condemn us unequivocally. Rather, Allah ﷻ loves that we turn to Him in repentance, engaging in regular self-accountability. Engaging in self-deprecation and thinking that our mistakes are the end of the world will create a loop of self-loathing that is not helpful and is, in fact, a trick of Shaytan to cause us to despair. The correct response is to ask Allah ﷻ for forgiveness. Al-Rahman (the Most Merciful) told us on many occasions how merciful He is; we also need to show some mercy to ourselves. Devaluing our essence because of our mistakes is denying our humanity. Abu Huraira (may Allah be pleased with him) reported: The Messenger of Allah ﷺ said, "By the One in whose hand is my soul, if you did not sin, Allah would replace you with people who would sin, and they would seek forgiveness from Allah and He would forgive them" (*Sahih Muslim*). Making mistakes and sinning are part of this human existence. The key is to turn back to Allah ﷻ again and again in repentance.

Finally, remember that everyone is walking with their own problems and mindsets formed by different experiences. If other people treat you unkindly or criticize you, don't interpret their treatment as a reflection of your worth. Instead, realize that they are simply not fortunate enough to be on a journey of self-awareness and improvement like you are. Indeed, we are precious, my sweet sister! Our Creator made us in the best way and gave us provisions and directions. He gave us the love and guidance of the greatest man to ever walk this earth, the Prophet ﷺ. Would He have done this if He didn't value us as His slaves?

Remember that your divorce doesn't define you. Your worth does not come from your husband, nor is it diminished by his absence in your life. You have the opportunity to grow and discover your true self and your strength. Embrace this time as a chance to reconnect with yourself and recognize the inherent value that lies within you.

CHALLENGE

Your challenge for this chapter is to rethink the value you assign to yourself and to acknowledge your worth as independent of your marriage or divorce and any perceived limitations. This is an opportunity to recognize the strengths and qualities that define you beyond your circumstances. If you haven't done so already, answer the questions that have preceded this chapter before you delve into the ones below.

1. How do you remind yourself that your worth isn't defined by your external circumstances or by others' opinions of you?

2. What practices or reminders help you resist devaluing yourself when you make mistakes or fall short?

3. What boundaries can you set to protect your self-worth from negative influences or self-doubt?

4. How can you stay grounded in your worth when facing criticism, judgment, or life challenges?

5. When challenges arise, how can you reframe them as opportunities to strengthen your sense of worth?

Part Two

FINDING THE PATH

6

Accepting *Qadr*

In the movie *Slumdog Millionaire*, an orphan from the slums of Mumbai becomes a contestant on the quiz show *Who Wants to Be a Millionaire?* After reaching the final question, Jamal is detained by the police, who can't believe that someone from the slums, with no formal education, could answer such difficult questions. Through a series of flashbacks during his interrogation, Jamal reveals how specific incidents in his life, many of them painful and seemingly random, provided him with the knowledge for each answer. Ultimately, what appeared to be a series of senseless hardships proved to be the stepping stones that led to his success. The producers of *Slumdog Millionaire* clearly understand the concept of *qadr* and managed to capture it brilliantly in the movie.

Qadr is the concept of predestination, or fate. The first object that Allah ﷻ created was the pen. He used the pen to record everything that has ever happened and will ever happen in a unique book called *al-Lawh al-Mahfuz*.

The Prophet ﷺ said, "First there was nothing. Then Allah created the throne, then the pen. Then Allah told it to write. The pen said, 'What should I write?' Allah said, 'Write the decree and details of everything that happens until the Day of Judgment'" (*Jami' al-Tirmidhi*).

Somewhere in the pages of *al-Lawh al-Mahfuz*, your name was written down alongside your husband's. And just as your marriage was decreed, so was your divorce!

The concept that everything is already written is an important part of our faith. Nothing happens unless Allah wills it to happen, and this is already written. In the famous hadith of Jibreel, the Prophet ﷺ explained *iman* (faith): that you "affirm your faith in Allah, in His angels, in His books, in His apostles, in the Day of Judgment, and you **affirm your faith in *al-qadr*, good and bad**."

Our belief in *qadr* is meant to help us through the hard times.

> *No calamity befalls anyone except by Allah's will.*
> *And whoever has faith in Allah, He will rightly*
> *guide their hearts through adversity. And Allah has*
> *perfect knowledge of all things. (Qur'an 64:11)*

The above verse shows us that if a person going through a difficulty knows it is coming from Allah ﷻ and accepts it, Allah ﷻ then guides their heart, providing much-needed relief. Descriptions of *qadr* may make us feel like we have no choice or that our actions don't matter, since everything is already decided. However, our actions and choices *do* matter, because *we* have no knowledge of what has already been written.

Qadr is about accepting Allah's names al-Khabeer (the All-Aware), al-Hakeem (the All-Wise), and al-Muqtadir (the All-Powerful One). Accepting that Allah's will—which is invariably good for us—prevails is in our best interest.

In a *hadith qudsi* (a narration attributed to Allah), Allah ﷻ tells us, "I am as My servant thinks of Me." We need to have good expectations of Allah ﷻ. If we can turn off the negative noise in our head and trust and expect good from Allah ﷻ, this shift in our perspective will help us to see things in a better light and to look for the benefits. In the Qur'an, Allah ﷻ calls Himself "the Best of Planners" (8:30). You may still find it difficult to accept His plan for you. You may still be saying to yourself things like, "If only I had done this or that," or "Why didn't it last?," or "Why did Allah allow this to happen to me?" Instead, here are some better questions to ask yourself:

- What have I learned from my experience that I can apply moving forward?
- What is a lesson that I may be missing?
- What have I gained from this experience?
- Could I have acted any differently considering the particular stage in my life and the information, experiences, and mindset I had at that point?
- As a result of this, have I changed or learned new ways to respond to similar situations in the future?

Regret

Soon after my divorce proceedings began, I started to feel debilitating regret for having married my former spouse in the first place. I berated myself for "making a mistake," replayed scenarios from our courting stage, and blamed myself for not having seen issues before they arose. I looked at my new baby and constantly felt my throat constrict and my eyes fill with tears. I felt like I had let her down the most. I had picked the wrong dad for her and couldn't forgive myself for failing her right from the start! I remembered reading about the rights of children over parents, and how their rights over us begin before they are even born, starting with the choice of a good partner to be their parent. I was convinced that I'd married the wrong guy and had a baby with the wrong man.

However, one imam, Imam Shadeed Muhammad, taught me a phrase that made all the difference: "moving forward." Instead of saying things such as "Why did I do that?" or "If only I had done that," I started asking myself, "If I am in a similar situation again, moving forward, what should I do?" or "Moving forward, how should I handle it?"

Playing out past scenarios in our heads is not useful. Not only do we not know what *could* have happened, we also do not know if the outcomes would have been what we wanted. There is no way for us to know what alternate realities could look like!

Allah ﷻ fully controls what happens in your life, and He also controls *when* it happens. Allah's timing is perfect. Before we begin healing and putting the puzzle pieces in place, we tend to punish ourselves for the things we overlooked or could have done better. We feel like beating ourselves up for not having made a better choice. We must trust that we did the best we could given who we were back then, the resources available to us, and the guidance Allah ﷻ provided for us.

Our job is to accept everything that has happened and focus on aligning ourselves with what pleases Allah 🕌.

There is a fable about a farmer whose horse ran away. When they heard about the missing horse, the farmer's neighbors told him, "We're so sorry, you have terrible luck!" and the farmer replied, "Maybe."

The next day, his horse returned, and it brought some wild horses with it. His neighbors came again and said, "Your horse came back and brought more! How lucky you are!" and the farmer again said, "Maybe."

A few days later, the farmer's son tried to break in one of the wild horses, but it threw him off, and the son broke his leg. The neighbors came back and said, "What terrible luck!" The farmer replied with another "maybe."

A few days later, army officials came to town to recruit soldiers into the army, but the farmer's son was not enlisted because of his broken leg. The neighbors again exclaimed how lucky the farmer was, and again he said, "Maybe."

This fable is particularly apt to our discussion. If we can develop an attitude of accepting that Allah's *qadr* is for the best, and say "*alhamdulillah*" ("Praise be to God") for everything, we will go far in living a peaceful life. We cannot change or escape our *qadr*. Ubadah ibn al-Samit said to his son (may Allah be pleased with them both), "Son! You will not taste the reality of faith until you know that what has come to you could not miss you, and that what has missed you could not come to you"(*Sunan Abu Dawud*).

Allah 🕌 decrees the events of our lives according to a plan. Sometimes we are fortunate enough to realize the wisdom in this lifetime. In my case, I became a completely new person after my divorce. Before, I was just cruising through life, deeply dissatisfied without even knowing why. After my divorce, Allah ﷻ taught me lesson after lesson, gave me a brand-new mindset, revealed my purpose and identity, and showed me what my shortcomings were. This book that I'm sharing with you now is just one positive result of that divorce. Before it, I wasn't willing to try a new route when driving, let alone try writing a book! Trust that there is a bigger wisdom behind things, even if you don't have the vantage point to appreciate it at this moment.

CHALLENGE

Your challenge in this chapter is to fully embrace the concept of acceptance, a crucial step in your journey moving forward.

1. What are some of your regrets from your marriage and divorce?

2. Moving forward, how will you do things differently? If you were to find yourself in the same situation you were in with your ex, given what you have now learned, what would your strategy be?

3. What are a few good things that came about as a result of your divorce?

4. One of the names of Allah is al-Qadir (the Most Powerful). When He decrees something, it comes into being without interruption or disturbance. Reflect on how this understanding of Allah's limitless capability and power influences your perception of your divorce, and write down your thoughts.

7

Accepting Your Ex-Husband

Terry McMillan's novel, *How Stella Got Her Groove Back,* is about a woman who finds love in her middle age with a dashing, much younger man who sweeps her off her feet. Interestingly, the book was based on the author's real-life story. However, things didn't pan out as she hoped. He ended up cheating on her, and they divorced.

Oprah Winfrey interviewed McMillan twice, with a notable gap between the interviews. In the first interview, McMillan's anger was so intense you could feel it through the screen. By the second interview, she was enveloped in peace. What happened? She had come to terms with her ex-husband's actions and with him as a person.

Any personal development coach will tell you that the quality of your life depends on the quality of your relationships. The most important relationships in your life are your relationships with

Allah ﷻ, yourself, and your family. Next come friends and community. This includes your ex-husband. If your relationship with him is contentious, it will affect your mental well-being. There are new rules to play by now: This man you were once so close to, whom you were physically intimate with, is now a non-*mahram* you need to cover yourself in front of. There are also a range of emotions that need to be dealt with, while simultaneously figuring out how to best show up as a coparent. **The goal now is to start accepting him as the flawed human he is.**

I spent a lot of time being angry at my ex-husband. I would get worked up thinking about some of the things he said and did. I would bristle at how he handled things. I fumed about his inability to see my point of view. Now, I can see that his perceived failings were not about me—there was no way he could have done and said the things that I wanted him to. He was, and is, his own person, who is very different from me; he has his own perspectives on life.

Due to my anger and resentment, I lost all respect for him, which showed in how I communicated. I struggled to speak to him normally—my tone of voice, my word choice, and my facial expressions all reflected my resentment. If I'm honest, disrespecting him made me feel empowered. However, that feeling was shallow and facetious; it was not real power. Eventually, I realized that this was not a character trait I wanted to embody; I finally wanted to forgive and let go.

In the McMillan interview, Oprah talked about someone she was angry with and holding a grudge against. She mentioned that she was surprised one day to randomly see the woman on the street, laughing as she walked into a luxury store. Oprah had expected her to be unhappy, but there she was, enjoying herself and buying luxury items. It's more common than you think to assume that if you are angry or holding a grudge against someone, they are also unhappy. In your mind's eye, you see them anchored to sadness as long as you remain angry.

As Oprah put it, forgiveness does not mean that what happened to you was OK—it is simply an acceptance that it happened. Now, what are you going to do about it?

Forgiveness is giving up the hope that the past could have been different. It is choosing to let go, so that the past can't hold you hostage. Forgiveness is not thinking about "woulda, coulda, shoulda." It is about being present right now, making decisions for right now, and moving forward.

I then asked myself, how do I take this explanation and understand it within the context of my *deen*?

I decided that forgiveness is **acting with *taqwa* (or mindfulness of Allah) and accepting *qadr*.** The Muslim is meant to always be mindful of Allah ﷻ—from how we enter the bathroom to how we carry ourselves in the grocery store and everything in between, including interacting with an ex. Forgiveness also means accepting that what has happened in your life was the *qadr* of Allah. It is embodying your belief in Allah's name, al-Adl (the Most Just). It is exercising *taqwa* in dealings with an ex-spouse, despite how you may feel.

The other person has nothing to do with letting go. It's about you allowing yourself to feel joy and freedom again, because whether or not you hold on to the pain or embrace joy, it doesn't change your ex's life. It's all about you, Sis. You're the one who can choose to release the anger, to break free.

Sometimes, though, we don't want to let go. Some people hold on to anger for decades. You've been hurt, and you've experienced disappointment, and those feelings are valid. But what I want you to do now is acknowledge those emotions, feel them, but don't allow them to consume you. Allow them to pass, so you can move forward.

In the following sections, we'll explore ideas to help you begin accepting your ex for who he is and find your own path to peace.

It Isn't Personal

Imagine a child who grew up watching his father abuse his mother. Throughout his childhood, he felt helpless listening to her pain without being able to intervene. Now, imagine that boy grows up. How do you think his childhood experiences will have shaped him? He might avoid marriage out of fear of becoming like his father. If he does get married, he is likely to repeat his father's actions because that's what he has learned. Unless he has a profound revelation or others teach him that what he witnessed was unhealthy behavior, this man will think of abuse as normal.

This story is an extreme example, but it demonstrates that we act based on what we know, our environment, and our upbringing. If this man goes on to treat his wife badly, his actions are a reflection of himself alone. They are not a reflection of his wife's value. He did not abuse her because she was a bad woman who deserved such treatment.

Let's say you grew up in a household where everyone ate when they wanted. However, your husband grew up with family dinners precisely at 6:00 p.m., and if his father was not home, his mother would not eat her meal. Family meals signified that they cared about each other. Now you are married to this man. One day, you get hungry and eat dinner before he gets home, not thinking anything of it. He may be hurt, however, because to him, dinner is not just a meal. You two just have different experiences and values.

Any behaviors that you and I encountered with our ex-husbands are not personal. It is not about you or me. He did certain things because that was what he knew to do, based on his experiences and upbringing. He has his own inner battles, his own way of thinking. He did not single you out and say, "OK, I am going to be amazing to everyone in my life, except her. I am going to make *her* miserable." Had he been married to Aisha, Zakia, or Farhana, his actions, thought process, and the lens through which he sees the world would be the same, because he is the same man!

Your ex-husband's behavior causes you pain because you may have internalized it as a reflection of your own worth. Subconsciously, you may have perceived his behavior toward you as a representation of the way the whole world sees you. Due to your experiences of injustice, you may have internalized the belief that you deserved it—and that everyone else thinks of you the same way and will treat you the same way too.

By understanding that it was never about you, you may be able to let go of the hurt and start seeing him in a neutral or even compassionate light.

Being Kind

Prophet Musa (peace be upon him) was sent to Fir'aun, who not only proclaimed himself God but also enslaved the Children of

Israel and murdered their babies. But despite Fir'aun's egregious sins, Allah ﷻ tells Musa to speak to him gently.

Allah ﷻ says, "Go to Pharaoh. He has tyrannized. But speak to him nicely. Perhaps he will remember, or have some fear" (Qur'an 20:43–44).

I was stunned when I first learned about this command. Then I thought to myself: If even Fir'aun, a baby-killing tyrant, was to be spoken to gently and treated in a civil, kind manner, then what about my ex-husband?

No matter how bad your ex might be, he is nowhere near as terrible as Fir'aun. Keeping this in mind, you need to approach your communication in a gentle manner. I know this can be tough, especially if he's the type who isn't fulfilling his duties to his children. However, your goal is acting in a way that will please Allah ﷻ, so aim for kindness. If that is too difficult, aim for the absence of unkindness. This is not to benefit him, or because he deserves your kindness; it's about protecting your heart and your emotional well-being. On the Day of Reckoning, you need to take a sound and clean heart back to Allah ﷻ, and you will immensely regret harming yourself by giving into the temptation to be mean to your ex-husband.

Not My Cup of Tea

I once attended a matchmaking event where we played a game arranging negative traits according to our tolerance levels. The lady next to me ranked "negativity" as her top intolerable trait and "pushover" at the very end. Surprised, I asked how she could tolerate a pushover. She replied, "I can't handle negative people at all.

That's why it's my priority." Meanwhile, "pushover" was first on my list!

This eye-opening exercise underscored the point that because it takes tolerance to stay married, one of the most important considerations for a lasting marriage is whether you can live with your partner's negative traits.

It's possible that your ex-husband's negative traits went against your core values and were deal-breakers for you. Perhaps you didn't know or trust yourself enough to recognize this before marriage. Maybe you were unaware of those traits or hoped he would change.

After the divorce, even if those traits were not the main reason for the separation, the aggravation you feel about them can be even worse. The heightened emotions and stress of the divorce process can magnify these traits, turning what once felt barely manageable into deep sources of frustration and bitterness. However, consider that everyone has negative traits. While they may feel overwhelmingly negative *to you*, remember that everyone has their own priorities and tolerances, and that your preferences do not make your ex-husband the worst person in the world. What is true in your eyes and from your point of view is not the only objective truth there is. Although the two of you are not compatible and not meant to be together, that does not make him the possessor of the worst negative traits in the world.

Ask Yourself . . .

What are some traits of your former spouse you could not tolerate? List them.

From what you know of him, can you pinpoint where his behavior may have stemmed from?

Ask a few sisters you know what negative traits they can and can't tolerate in a marriage. It will show you how different we all are!

Your Ex as a Father

Some find it easy to fulfill the rights of others while others may struggle. Don't despair if your ex-husband doesn't support his children financially. It is his own test from Allah for him to contend with on the Day of Judgment. It's not your responsibility to make someone else fulfill their obligations. We are limited in how much we can influence others to do what we want them to do. Even the Prophet ﷺ could not convince his beloved uncle to accept Islam.

However, his behavior is a test for you as well. Does this adversity change you from being a generous person to someone callous and vindictive? Or do you move through it with grace and pass your own test? While you may feel angry or helpless, recognize that Allah ﷻ chose your child's father in His ultimate wisdom. The rest of it is a test for you to navigate through. Allah is the ultimate provider of provisions and safety, the source of *rizq*. If it is meant to come through your ex-husband, it will. If he isn't stepping up, he will answer for his failure, and your *rizq* and that of your children will still come through the means Allah deems best.

Remember the story of Musa and Khidr from Surat al-Kahf. Musa (peace be upon him) sought knowledge and wisdom from Khidr (peace be upon him), but throughout their travels, he witnessed Khidr engaging in seemingly unjust actions that he could not comprehend. For example, Khidr damaged a boat belonging to a fisherman who helped them. Musa reacted with shock and indignation, questioning Khidr's motives and judgment. However, as the story unfolded, Musa gradually learned that there were deeper reasons behind Khidr's actions, which were guided by a divine wisdom that Musa wasn't privy to. For instance, the boat Khidr damaged was saved from being seized by a tyrant king, thus saving the boat owner's livelihood.

Through this experience, Musa learned important lessons about trust, humility, and the limitations of human understanding. He came to realize that true wisdom often lies beyond superficial appearances and requires patience and faith to fully comprehend.

The lack of financial support from your ex might be a form of goodness or protection, a wisdom from Allah ﷻ that you haven't yet been made aware of. If you have taken measures to get your *haqq* (rights) and it still does not happen, then leave it to Allah. It is better to sincerely believe in Allah's ultimate justice, continue to treat your former spouse with respect and civility, and leave the door open for the children to have a relationship with their father.

If he is not regularly seeing them or showing up emotionally, prioritize your mental health and focus on being the best mom you can be. Trying to be both mother and father is not only unrealistic but also detrimental. It will only stretch you beyond your capacity and compromise your role as a mother.

The sooner you accept him as the father he is (and not the father you wish he would be), the sooner you can be fully available for your kids as they cope with his absence. Direct them to Allah's love for them, and gently teach them that the limitations of human love do not apply to Allah. Additionally, utilize the exercises in this chapter to overcome resentment toward your ex-husband. This will make it easier for your children to come to you with their feelings and not feel conflicted about missing him. Even when something remains unspoken, children can sense it, so make sure your acceptance and neutrality toward him are genuine.

This journey of letting go of lingering hurt is incredibly challenging, but it will ultimately lead to healthier dynamics and a more stable future for you and your children. Years down the road, you will feel grateful for the intentional effort you put into making the best of your situation.

Now that we've addressed accepting your ex-husband for who he is, we'll shift the focus back to you in the next chapter and begin the process of taking accountability.

CHALLENGE

Your challenge for this chapter is to see and accept your ex-husband as the flawed human he is, not who you want him to be. This will lead you to a sense of peace. The exercises for this chapter are especially important; the trajectory of your future can improve significantly with the sense of peace that comes from accepting him. Be patient with yourself and take your time to internalize the lessons. Feel free to redo this chapter's exercises again and again if needed.

1. What is one small change you can make to communicate with your ex more kindly?

2. What is one healthy way to process tough emotions, instead of venting to friends or family?

3. What helps you remember that your ex is simply a means through which Allah provides for your children?

4. Take a moment to reflect on Allah's names al-Razzaq (the Provider) and al-Wadud (the Loving). How do these names shape your approach to healing?

5. What makes it hard to let go of certain hurts? What would make letting go easier for you?

6. What would forgiving your ex look and feel like for you?

8

Taking Accountability

One of the most daunting yet transformative journeys we can take in the aftermath of a marriage is the journey of considering our own role in its unraveling. It's a process that demands courage—the willingness to confront our own actions, decisions, and attitudes. It requires navigating layers of emotions (including guilt, regret, and denial), but it leads to deep insights and personal growth. It isn't easy, but it clears the way toward healing and healthier relationships in the future.

If our divorce is to serve us moving forward, we need to assess ourselves fairly and honestly. We need to be open, face uncomfortable truths, and see what our contributions to the situation were. If we take the necessary steps to do this, Allah will help us by changing things for the better as well. *Muhasabah* is self-accountability or self-assessment. It is evaluating our failures and taking account of ourselves. It is honest self-criticism that our *deen* encourages. If we find that we did something good, we need to continue doing it consistently. If we find that we did something bad, we need to change course and correct ourselves.

I am not a blameless victim, and neither are you.* This is not to belittle what happened to you in your marriage. "What about the injustices *I* faced?" you may ask. No one is denying or invalidating what happened. Ultimately, each person will be answerable for their own shortcomings and sins. However, we need to ask ourselves what role we played and where we might have done better.

While in sessions, my coach repeatedly told me that I had made my own choices and that I had a role to play both in my marriage and in my divorce. At the time, I felt too hurt and victimized, and the lesson just didn't sink in. The penny only dropped two years later, on a night when I wasn't even thinking about divorce. One evening, I glanced at my daughter twisting puzzle pieces, carefully trying each one, determined to make them fit on the board. While watching her, it hit me—I wasn't just a piece in my own life puzzle, moved by circumstances; I had a role in where each piece would fall.

I hadn't been a passive observer in my marriage or my divorce. I had chosen him, and I had chosen to leave. My life wasn't just happening to me; I *had* a choice! I *had* a part to play! I wasn't merely watching things as they happened; I was an active participant in what happened.

_____

*This book addresses women exiting nonabusive relationships. Not all of the content will apply to survivors of domestic violence and extreme abuse.

Sis, we had a choice in the matter. We chose to marry our spouses. Now, we can choose to move forward and learn from the divorce too. Just as he did not drag you to the masjid to sign the *nikah* contract, he cannot force you into a corner and make you stay miserable and lost either. The key is with you to heal and move forward. Hindsight is 20/20, and while it may take time to even admit that you played a role in both your marriage and your divorce, as long as you continue to be willing to reflect, Allah will open the doors of understanding for you.

But be sure to show yourself empathy when it comes to your choices and your mistakes—you didn't know better at the time. At the end of the day, even if you had done all the research in the world, prayed, and known yourself intimately, the outcome would still not be in your hands.

The goal is to get yourself out of the victim mentality. Blaming the ex-husband, the family, and everyone else is a weak position to be in. When we believe in our own victimhood, we become puppets with no agency. We need to take responsibility for our role too. Then, we can show ourselves compassion, accept our choices, and extract the necessary lessons. We need to know ourselves intimately by understanding our thought processes, past wounds, triggers, and more. Taking accountability empowers us to evolve beyond our past choices and take constructive steps forward. Umar (may Allah be pleased with him) described the transformative nature of accountability:

> *Assess yourselves before you are assessed, and weigh your deeds before they are weighed for you. Adorn yourselves for the Day of Resurrection, for judgment will be light on the Day of Judgment for the one who judged himself in the world.*

How do we start taking accountability for ourselves? It begins with understanding who we are, and how we came to be the way we are. The following sections discuss a few ways to reflect on our past and the choices we made.

Your Upbringing

One of the things that can have an impact on your relationships is your childhood and upbringing. You can begin to think about this by reflecting on the environment in which you were raised. This examination is crucial in recognizing how your experiences shaped the partner you choose, your marriage, and even how you handled divorce. Reflecting on the family dynamics you observed and the values instilled in you can reveal patterns in your choices and behaviors. Acknowledging these influences is about broadening your understanding of yourself; it's not about casting blame.

Consider the dynamics between your parents or guardians. Next, assess the values and beliefs instilled in you during your formative years. In Islam, the importance of justice, mercy, and consultation (*shura*) within the family is emphasized. Reflect on how these principles were modeled in your household. Did you witness fairness and compassion in your parents' interactions? Were your opinions valued and considered? Additionally, examine your responses to conflict and stress. If your childhood involved witnessing or experiencing conflict, you might have developed certain coping mechanisms, such as avoidance, aggression, or seeking external validation.

Ask Yourself . . .

How would you describe the relationship between your parents or guardians when you were growing up?

What were the core values and beliefs emphasized in your household?

How have these values shaped your expectations and behaviors in your relationship?

How did you typically respond to conflict or stress?

Have these mechanisms evolved? How do they manifest in your current interactions and responses within relationships?

Ignoring Intuition

Intuition is a natural instinct or feeling that we can't always justify rationally, but it often carries valuable insights. Allah ﷻ tells us in the Qur'an that there is indeed a form of discerning internal guidance:

> *Oh you who believe! If you obey and fear Allah, He will*
> *grant you* furqan *[(a criterion to judge between right and*
> *wrong), or* (makhraj, *i.e., a way for you to get out from every*
> *difficulty)], and will expiate for you your sins, and forgive you;*
> *and Allah is the Owner of the great bounty. (Qur'an 8:29)*

Too often, we ignore this inner knowledge and dismiss it without reflection. It is important to acknowledge and explore these feelings, especially when making major life decisions like choosing a spouse. Pray *istikhara*, consult trusted people, and seek evidence (or the lack of it) to confirm your intuition. But don't brush your intuition under the rug or pretend the feeling never surfaced.

Many women ignore their own intuition and tell themselves that *they* are the problem. "I do not feel right about this, but he comes from a good family and is a *hafidh* (someone who memorized the Qur'an)" or "Something about this doesn't feel right but I must just be overreacting or nervous."

Many of the issues that made me want to end my marriage were present in the courting stage; I just failed to recognize them or act according to my values. Later, I could not forgive myself. I was angry at myself for my "stupidity," but that's giving myself too much credit. I am human and make mistakes and don't know everything. Only Allah ﷻ has perfect knowledge of the future. If that particular person had not become my ex-husband, it would have been someone else, as long as there was a lesson to be learned.

Intuition is a God-given gift. Forgive yourself for having shunned your gift. Add learning how to trust yourself and listen to your intuition to the list of good things that came out of your divorce.

Ask Yourself . . .

Were there any warning signs that you ignored in the courtship phase?

Why do you think you chose to ignore them?

What was your internal dialogue at the time?

How can you learn to trust yourself and your intuition?

Your Shadow

In psychology, the "shadow" refers to the unconscious part of our character or personality that does not align with the ideal version of what we're aiming for. Like an actual shadow, however, it isn't necessarily negative. It represents something hidden in the dark—something we tend to reject or conceal within ourselves. According to Jungian analyst, Aniela Jaffe, the shadow is the "sum of all personal and collective psychic elements which, because of their incompatibility with the chosen conscious attitude, are denied expression in life."

Shedding light on your shadows is a necessary part of knowing yourself better, accepting your whole self, and integrating your sense of self in a more holistic manner. One of the best ways to do this is to examine the person you married.

The reality is that we are attracted to people who are similar or familiar to us in some manner. The Prophet ﷺ said, "Souls are like conscripted soldiers; those whom they recognize, they get along with, and those whom they do not recognize, they will not get along with" (*Sahih al-Bukhari*). In what ways is your ex similar to you? Think about what initially attracted you to your ex-husband. Was there something in him that reflected a part of you—whether positive or negative? What was it?

The negative aspects you saw in him may have been a mirror to your own "shadow self," reflecting qualities within yourself that you may not have fully acknowledged.

Consider the qualities that you didn't like about him, and be vulnerable enough to examine whether you share those traits as well. Once you recognize the shadows, you can learn to accept them, and there won't be a need to feel defensive or triggered by those things. For example, you may describe your ex as a "control freak"; you hated how he always wanted things in a specific way. In contrast, you are messy. On the surface, you look like opposites, but perhaps you both grew up in a tumultuous home and had an unpredictable childhood. While his reaction is to control his immediate environment, yours is an inability to keep anything organized. His need for order may trigger a deep-seated shame and unprocessed trauma you feel around your own upbringing. Things have a way of unraveling once you pull on the loose thread.

Allah is al-Tawwab (the Acceptor of Repentance). There is a key word there to pay attention to—"acceptor." Allah ﷻ not only accepts our repentance for our sins, He also accepts *us*. Allah accepts us as we are, with our quirks, our shortcomings, and our unique way of being. Can *we* accept the parts of ourselves that we don't necessarily like? If Allah ﷻ accepts it all, so can we.

Your Triggers

Years ago, I listened to a podcast where the guest discussed feeling agitated if his wife wasn't there as he came through the door. I immediately judged him. What if she was busy doing something in the back of the house?

It turned out that as a little boy, he came home from school one day, and his mom had left, never to come back. It scarred him for life, triggering an unwelcome reaction whenever his wife was absent.

What are some things that trigger you? What induces a sense of discomfort? For example, a woman may feel triggered and react when others talk about cooking or how important it is for a woman to know how to cook. If she is at a gathering and someone is praising a dish made by another sister, this might trigger a sense of feeling personally attacked. She may be harboring a sense of shame about how mediocre her own cooking skills are. How does this sister move forward? She can decide to accept and embrace her level, she can decide to learn how to be a better cook, or she can decide to be happy with her other skills and just not focus on cooking! When she accepts this aspect of herself, she will no longer be triggered when she hears comments that are not even directed at her at all.

Ask Yourself . . .

What were some things that triggered you about your ex-husband?

What do you think the root cause of the trigger was? Did it play any role in your divorce?

How will you handle the trigger moving forward?

Being Introspective

There is nothing in this world more effective than marriage, divorce, and children to bring the deepest parts of ourselves to light. Dormant places we didn't even know existed are awakened thanks to intimate and difficult relationships. Use this to your advantage!

If your ex-husband described your role in the relationship in a way that you would consider negative, ask yourself honestly if you *did* embody those characteristics. Be curious and explore the possibilities. Remember, just because someone says something does not make it a fact. You do not have to believe him automatically, as he could be projecting his own issues (his own shadow) onto you.

However, don't just dismiss his point of view out of hand; take the time to consider it seriously.

Maybe your contribution to the end of the marriage was that you chose to marry him in the first place, even though you suspected you might not be compatible. Or maybe you were not emotionally available, and you are now realizing how that affected his actions. Remember, this is about knowing yourself on a deeper level, not about *his* mistakes and his role.

Identifying Cognitive Dissonance

In psychology, cognitive dissonance is the mental discomfort experienced by a person who simultaneously holds two or more contradictory beliefs, ideas, or values. Because this situation is uncomfortable, we try to reduce the dissonance by using self-justification.

Here is a simple example: You buy an expensive winter coat in the middle of summer. You do not need it; you have lots of coats already. There is little closet space, and you have been wanting to save money and control your spending. As a result, you feel some internal discomfort about the purchase, because it illustrates a contradiction between your values and your actions. This feeling is cognitive dissonance. Because we need psychological consistency to function well in life, self-justification swoops in with an excuse to save the day: "That coat was on sale, and it's such high quality! Besides, I'll need an extra coat if something happens to the ones I already own." You tell yourself a story to quiet your guilty conscience, attempting to make your actions appear in line with your values. Understanding how cognitive dissonance works is key in this journey of knowing ourselves better. We can not only see the inner workings of ourselves but also understand others when they display cognitive dissonance.

When we do anything that harms someone else—getting them in trouble or verbally disrespecting them, for example—our cognitive dissonance causes us to feel the need to justify what we did. People accused of torturing others often do not display guilt due to cognitive dissonance, because they have created a story to convince themselves that their victims deserved it.

Cognitive dissonance is powerful! A newly married couple who are still in the honeymoon phase justify each other's short-comings positively. For example, in the beginning, a wife might think "How cute that he is so protective of me!"; a few years later, this turns into "What a jealous control freak!"

Here are more examples:

- A mother tells her children's father that he cannot visit this weekend, but she knows they miss him. She reduces dissonance by saying, "They don't want to miss their cousin's birthday on Sunday. Besides, he is a bad influence on them."
- A woman notices that the man she is considering marrying is stingy. She quiets her mind by saying, "It's good that he is careful with his money, he is saving for our future."
- A father may not visit his children for months. He reduces dissonance by saying, "Their mom's family is big, the kids will be fine. Besides, she always makes the visits awkward."

Facing the dissonance between our ideals and actions can be uncomfortable, but it's where real change begins. By honestly confronting these inner conflicts, we create space to align our values and choices.

All in all, embrace self-reflection and accountability. By honestly assessing your actions, you pave the way for genuine personal growth, a crucial step toward becoming the person you aspire to be.

CHALLENGE

Your challenge for this chapter is to take ownership of your role. This requires bravery as you confront yourself. It may take time to overcome resistance and be truly honest, so be patient with yourself. Reflect on all the questions you've encountered in this chapter, either here or in your workbook, which has them all compiled in one place.

1. What small changes can you start to make to avoid passing down unhelpful beliefs about love, marriage, or conflict to future generations?

2. What's one way you can build a habit of listening to your intuition and judgment, even when it feels uncomfortable?

3. What steps can you take to recognize and work with insecurities or fears, so they don't drive your future decisions?

4. What are some things your former spouse did that did not initially bother you only to become huge issues later?

5. What are some ways cognitive dissonance shows up in your current relationship as coparents?

9

Surrendering to His Plan

I once went on *umrah* (the minor pilgrimage). It was a short trip, with only four days in Mecca. I wanted to make a second *umrah* and woke up on my third day with that intention set. Unfortunately, it looked to be a busy day with a tight schedule; our group was leaving the next day and there was a requirement to test for Covid before departing. At the time, *umrah* was via appointment only, and mine was set for after Maghrib. That meant I needed to finish Dhuhr at Masjid al-Haram, go back to the hotel, wait for the PCR people, shower, and find a taxi to take me to the *miqat* (the location from which an *umrah* begins) and back, all before 'Asr.

Strangely enough, I wasn't worried for a moment, and it was thanks to the *barakah* (blessings) of the sacred cities. I made the intention to do a second *umrah* and did not think about it again. At home, I would have been fretting and anxious, calculating how long it would take me to do one task after another, worrying about whether the PCR guys would be on time, if there would be traffic, you name it. A vicious cycle of planning, predicting, and obsessing over the tiniest detail. I would have been running through various disaster scenarios in my head all day. Instead, it all worked out beautifully. I prayed Dhuhr, walked into the lobby, and the PCR people were already there. They took my sample immediately, and then I went back upstairs for a shower. When I walked out of the hotel, there was already a taxi by the door, as if waiting for me. I made it back with plenty of time to spare before 'Asr!

How can we bring the type of surrender I experienced that morning to our day-to-day lives?

Confronting Loss of Control with *Tawakkul*

When I first decided to go to court, I was looking for justice. I was incredibly hurt and in pain. My ex-husband did not want us to go to court; he implored me to settle things outside of court. I wanted an outside party to witness my pain and deliver justice, so I refused. I also wanted to go to court simply because he did not want to—an attempt to get back at him, perhaps?

Instead, the process was like a suicide bomb. Sure, he was suffering through the process, but so was I. I learned too late that the only winners in court are the legal help we hire. Not only did I *not* get justice, but the years to come were riddled with anxiety and stress, going back and forth for court proceedings.

My heart screamed every time I went to court and the judge didn't see things my way. The procedure made me feel unsafe; I experienced an utter loss of control. I was on an unpredictable rollercoaster, depending on the lawyers and court officials in a way that required me to simply watch as they did what they thought fit. My lawyer wouldn't return calls for weeks at a time, multiplying the stress tenfold. For a long time, I struggled to surrender to Allah's will, often holding on to hopes for specific outcomes and feeling disappointed when they didn't happen. I had not yet learned to surrender, to truly let go of the desire to control everything around me.

While routines and predictability are necessary in life, they can create a false sense of being in charge. Often, our attempts to control situations arise from an underlying fear that if we don't, what we fear will indeed come to pass.

Tawakkul is the act of absolutely trusting in and relying on Allah. Even when you're weighed down by anxiety or uncertainty, *tawakkul* lifts you, bringing peace in knowing that Allah's plan is always unfolding as it should. As the Qur'an reminds us, "Allah loves those who put their trust in Him" (3:159). While you may understand intellectually that trusting Allah is essential, how do you truly feel it in your heart? The foundation of that trust lies in truly knowing Allah. Just like we learn to trust people based on their reliability and character, we build trust in Allah as we come to understand His names and attributes—the Creator, the All-Wise, the All-Powerful. As your understanding deepens through your *deen*, this trust grows, bringing a steady calm, even in life's storms.

Despite your desires for a specific outcome, you never truly know what is best for you. Only Allah possesses that knowledge, as He teaches us in the Qur'an: "But perhaps you hate a thing and it is good for you; and perhaps you love a thing and it is bad for you. And Allah knows, while you know not" (Qur'an 2:216). What you can control is your response to whatever comes your way and the meaning you attach to these challenges.

Using *Istikhara* to Pray for Guidance

A shaykh once shared a story about a car trip he took with his son that ended in an accident. The car flipped over, leaving them suspended upside down, waiting for help. At that moment, the shaykh reassured his son, saying, "Don't worry, son, I prayed *istikhara* before we left." I was floored when I heard this. I could not fathom this type of certainty in one's decisions. I definitely was not someone who prayed *istikhara* before deciding to jump in my car and go somewhere.

During my divorce, I constantly sought advice from others, desperate for guidance. One friend repeatedly urged me to pray *salat al-istikhara*. *Salat al-istikhara* is a prayer for guidance, a check-in with Allah ﷻ to make sure a decision or action is aligned with His will. Initially, this frustrated me, but eventually, I took her advice and began praying *salat al-istikhara* before moving forward with any decision.

The Prophet ﷺ advised us to pray *salat al-istikhara* to seek Allah's guidance for all decisions in our lives, even in the simplest of matters. *Istikhara* is two rak'as of prayer, followed by a specific *du'a*. Pray *istikhara* for every decision you make during your divorce proceedings and afterwards.

There are many benefits to this practice. For one, it will slow you down, keeping you from making decisions based on hasty, knee-jerk reactions. Instead, they will be well-thought-out and not impulsively based on high emotions.

Alongside praying *istikhara*, ask the advice of trusted people who have Islamic knowledge and life experience. They will likely have insights that didn't occur to you.

Another benefit of praying *istikhara* is that you will feel more content with the outcome of your situation, even if it isn't what you wanted. After all, you checked in with your Creator and sought His pleasure in your action, so your heart will find it easier to accept and cope with whatever unfolds.

Instructions for Performing Istikhara

1. **Make a decision.** Before performing *istikhara*, make your choice clear in your mind regarding the matter you are seeking guidance about.
2. **Pray two rak'as.** Offer two units (rak'as) of voluntary prayer. This prayer can be performed at any time of the day, except during prohibited times.
3. **Recite the *du'a*.** After completing the prayer, recite the *istikhara du'a* sincerely, asking Allah for guidance.

The Dua

اللّٰهُمَّ إِنِّي أَسْتَخِيرُكَ بِعِلْمِكَ وَأَسْتَقْدِرُكَ بِقُدْرَتِكَ، وَأَسْأَلُكَ مِنْ فَضْلِكَ الْعَظِيمِ، فَإِنَّكَ تَقْدِرُ وَلَا أَقْدِرُ وَتَعْلَمُ وَلَا أَعْلَمُ وَأَنْتَ عَلَّامُ الْغُيُوبِ اللّٰهُمَّ إِنْ كُنْتَ تَعْلَمُ أَنَّ هَذَا الْأَمْرَ خَيْرٌ لِي فِي دِينِي وَمَعَاشِي وَعَاقِبَةِ أَمْرِي فَاقْدُرْهُ لِي وَيَسِّرْهُ لِي ثُمَّ بَارِكْ لِي فِيهِ وَإِنْ كُنْتَ تَعْلَمُ أَنَّ هَذَا الْأَمْرَ شَرٌّ لِي فِي دِينِي وَمَعَاشِي وَعَاقِبَةِ أَمْرِي فَاصْرِفْهُ عَنِّي وَاصْرِفْنِي عَنْهُ، وَاقْدُرْ لِي الْخَيْرَ حَيْثُ كَانَ ثُمَّ أَرْضِنِي بِهِ

Oh Allah, I seek Your guidance [in making a choice] by virtue of Your knowledge, and I seek ability by virtue of Your power, and I ask You of Your great bounty. You have power, and I do not. You know, and I know not, and You are the Knower of the unseen.

Oh Allah, if You know that this matter [mention the thing to be decided] is good for me in my religion, my livelihood, my worldly affairs, and in the hereafter, then decree it for me, make it easy for me, and bless it for me. And if You know that this matter is bad for me in my religion, my livelihood, my worldly affairs, and in the hereafter, then turn it away from me and turn me away from it, and decree for me the good wherever it may be and make me content with it.

Acting with *Taqwa*

Abu Salih reported that a man said to Abu Huraira (may Allah be pleased with him), "What is *taqwa* [God-fearing mindfulness]?" Abu Huraira said, "Have you ever taken a thorny path?" The man said yes. Abu Huraira said, "What did you do?" The man said, "If I saw thorns, I would avoid them, pass over them, or stop short of them." Abu Huraira said, "That is *taqwa*" (*al-Zuhd al-kabir*).

When dealing with the legal separation of assets or figuring out how to handle your children's future, remember the example of walking through a thorny field. Imagine your anger, your family's and ex's behavior, the mean words, and the judges and lawyers who do not understand you or see your view as the thorny field. Make sure you navigate carefully through this field. At the end of the day, the outcome of what you will find on the other side of the field is not known. But if you navigate the thorny field carefully, your skin and clothes will stay protected. Similarly, your heart will remain clear, allowing you to discover peace and other beautiful things, whatever they may be, at the end of the field. You may find this peace and unexpected positivity in this world, or your reward may only be manifest in the next life. Or you may be unhappy with the outcome in this world, but that's when you whip out the patience pill. Or perhaps things work out better than you ever could have imagined, and that is when you bring out the gratitude and humility pill. Either way, you will be rewarded.

In moments when we get the positive outcomes we desire, we should remember how the Prophet ﷺ entered Mecca. After all the humiliation and torture he had endured, he was humble in victory. He rode into the city surrounded by people who had caused him unimaginable pain, but his head was bowed and he was engaged in *dhikr*. He did not gloat or taunt his former enemies, even though he had every right to. We should embody the Prophet's humility and dignity. We must thank Allah ﷻ and move forward with grace.

In moments when the outcome is not what we desired, it is completely normal to feel down, but remember that not everything is as it seems. You prayed *istikhara*, you sought counsel, and things didn't work out the way you wanted, but have faith that Allah gave you and the children the thing you needed. Maybe this outcome is meant to test you, or it is to elevate you, or it is a form of protection and goodness that you don't understand right now. Know that we can act with *ihsan* (excellence) and sincerity, but we can't control the outcome. Allah ﷻ will reward us if we make sure our actions are in accordance with what He has prescribed.

Keeping Intentions Pure

For a long time, when my ex-husband would start a text with "Assalamu alaikum," I had a hard time returning the *salam*. My anger and hatred would not allow me to wish him peace even verbally. I would write back, "Hello." It bothered me, but I just couldn't bring myself to do it. There wasn't a single shred of goodwill left in me. After a while, a friend helped me reframe it. I am not responding to his *salam*s because I personally wish him peace. I am responding because it is what Allah ﷻ and my Prophet ﷺ commanded me to do; I will respond appropriately to honor and obey *them*.

Ultimately, it was not about my feelings or my ex's; rather, I had to learn how to respond in a way that honors my relationship with Allah ﷻ. That mindset shift helped a lot. Instead of agonizing over how to respond, I turned to a higher chain of command—Allah. And that was a relief! It gave me a framework from which to act. It can work for other situations too. If you feel confused or lost about a decision or response, defer to a higher authority and ask "What does Allah ﷻ want from me now?"

CHALLENGE

Your challenge for this chapter is to let go of your current expectations with your divorce and to surrender to and consult Allah ﷻ. This is especially important if you are currently engaged in a court case with your ex-spouse.

1. Describe a situation in your divorce where the outcome was or is entirely beyond your control.

2. What does releasing your need for control and fully surrendering to Allah ﷻ look like for you?

3. How would truly surrendering to Allah ﷻ feel emotionally?

4. What pending decision in your divorce could benefit most from practicing *tawakkul* and entrusting your matters to Allah?

5. What are some current situations in your life where praying *istikhara* could bring you relief and clarity?

10

Embracing Gratitude

first used the Kia Soul as a vacation rental a few years ago. I'd never seen it before and asked the car rental people if it was a new release. They told me it wasn't! After returning it, I realized the car is more common than I first thought. I began seeing it everywhere, at least once a day, if not more. Did they suddenly flood the markets with Kias? No. I just wasn't aware of it before, but now that my mind was made aware of it, I began to notice it. I would smile every time I saw one of those models on the street, because it reminded me of my vacation bliss.

I had a similar experience when I got pregnant with my little girl. Suddenly, pregnant women were everywhere—in line at the grocery store, crossing the street, waiting at the bank—each with a different-sized bump, as if the whole world were expecting. They seemed to have come out of nowhere and flooded the streets. I had never seen so many pregnant women in my life!

This is called the Baader-Meinhof Phenomenon, or "frequency bias." The brain realizes something is important or interesting to you, so it adjusts its filters and brings it to your attention when it occurs. We can use this phenomenon along with gratitude to increase the good things in our lives by priming our brains to focus on good things.

One of the most powerful tools we have during divorce is gratitude. Despite the deep pain, gratitude offers us relief and comfort. It's like enjoying chicken soup when you have the flu—even though you're still feeling unwell, that soup can make you feel so much better. In the same way, gratitude serves as chicken soup for your heart.

As you are walking through your house, you stub your toe. The pain is intense and it's all you think about at that moment. But does that mean your other healthy organs are not there? Even if you don't realize it at that exact moment, there are many good things in your day and in your life that are worth noticing. Maybe it's the rare but real moments of rest, like a solid night's sleep that helps you recharge. Or a close friend who sticks around, showing up just to listen. There might be small comforts you hadn't thought much about before, like the calm that comes from stepping outside for a few minutes or simply having a warm drink to start your day. And even though this experience is hard, it's okay to recognize that, in some ways, it could have been worse.

When we are going through something difficult, it is easy to forget everything good and focus on just the one issue. If we ignore our blessings, then we will not see them even though they are still there. If we focus on our blessings, then they will become more apparent as we give them more attention.

By virtue of how the *dunya* is structured, there is always going to be hardship. Don't tell yourself, "Let this divorce be over first, and *then* I will be grateful." The time to look for blessings is now, even while you're in the deep end of the pool, dealing with the heartache and pain of divorce. When it feels like someone is squeezing the very life out of you, and you're overwhelmed with hurt and disbelief, gratitude can help anchor you to the reality that all is not lost.

Allah ﷻ tells us that along with hardship, there is ease. Never forget that there really is ease and blessing alongside the hardship we're dealing with.

With.

Not after!

> ***With** hardship comes ease. (Qur'an 94:5)*

The very next verse repeats this reminder:

> *Surely with [that] hardship comes [more] ease. (Qur'an 94:6)*

Some scholars of the Arabic language* even say that the Arabic word used for "ease" is plural, to indicate that, along with the hardship, there are multiple blessings. "Ease" in our lives is not a singular occurrence; the ease in our lives is multifold and plentiful, *alhamdulillah.*

---

*Dr. Mustafa Khattab, translator of the *Clear Qur'an*, explains this in the digital version of the *Clear Qur'an*.

It took two long years after my divorce for me to truly experience the sweetness of gratitude. I joined a challenge to start gratitude journaling by writing ten things each day for a month. Initially, I was skeptical that it would bring any real change. I struggled to find anything to be grateful for, but someone in the group suggested starting with the basics. So, I began by acknowledging simple things like the pen I was using and the chair I was sitting in as I wrote. For days, I kept adding more simple things (like the coffee I had or even the cup!), eventually moving on to bigger examples of what I was grateful for.

Sometime later, an incident happened that showed me the difference the journaling was making behind the scenes. I was having an exhausting day and did not want to leave the house, but groceries needed to be bought. As I left the store and started unloading the cart, resentment and self-pity started bubbling up to the surface, and then the gratitude stopped it. I started thinking, "At least I can afford to buy groceries and feed my child!" and "At least I don't have to worry about drama with a crazy ex!" This change in thought was not a conscious effort; it happened organically. I was so surprised at my lack of misery and marveled at the miracle unfolding. That moment showed me that consciously practicing gratitude can change the way we perceive events in our lives, even when we're not actively trying. Over time, we find that, even on tough days, we naturally shift toward finding positive aspects of a situation without having to make a conscious effort. We automatically appreciate a small kindness from someone or the beauty of a sunny day, even when we're otherwise feeling stressed or overwhelmed.

Have you ever planted a flower? If you water it, remove the weeds, and make sure it has nutritious soil, it will grow. That is the rule of this world. Whatever we give attention to grows. The grass is greener on the side you water. That's why in the Islamic tradition we are taught to do *dhikr* and be more grateful. The more we think of Allah's blessings, the more we feel grateful. The more you nurture and pay attention to your anger and pain, the more it grows. What do you want to fill your heart with? Gratitude, love, and *dhikr*? Or anger, resentment, and hate? Make a conscious choice to embrace the positive.

CHALLENGE

Your challenge for this chapter is to refresh and deepen your sense of gratitude and look for the small and big signs that demonstrate Allah's love for you.

1. What are five blessings you are experiencing right now? Start with something very simple—it can be something as basic as the chair you are sitting on right this very moment.

2. Consider something you often take for granted. How would your life be different without it? How can you express more gratitude for this blessing?

3. How could your divorce be even more challenging? Consider situations you don't face but could have, which would make it that much worse. What aspects of your current reality do you find yourself appreciating when you consider how much worse things could have been?

Part Three

EMBRACING
THE JOURNEY

11

Self-Care

Some of us live by the mantra "You can rest when you're dead." This relentless mindset often comes at the expense of our well-being and pushes us to the brink. It's usually only after a serious diagnosis or a major life event that we start questioning this approach. This is what happened to a friend of mine. After years of dismissing the warning signs, she faced a health crisis that forced her to reevaluate her priorities. Instead of returning to her old habits, she began embracing self-care and learned to set boundaries that honored her needs.

You are the CEO of your life and home, and you don't have to wait until you are completely burned-out to start taking self-care seriously. Prioritizing your well-being will help you maintain a calm and composed presence in your home, which is essential for a fulfilling life.

Often, we feel guilty and selfish for taking even a few minutes to ourselves. We may feel like it is taking something away from someone else. But this ties into the issue of self-worth: Sometimes we feel so unimportant that we don't feel we deserve self-care. Sometimes we are so disconnected from ourselves that we don't know who we are right now or how to nurture ourselves.

You are not less important than anyone else. You are worthy of self-care not only to show up with excellence for others but also simply because you are worthy and deserving of it just by virtue of being human. In fact, the Prophet ﷺ said, "Your wife has a right on you, your guest has a right on you, **your self has a right on you**. You should fast and [sometimes] not fast, and [you should both] pray and sleep" (*Sunan Abu Dawud*).

As we saw in Chapter 3, we are more than just physical beings. Contrary to popular belief, self-care is not solely about pampering our bodies. By identifying which part of us needs care, we can focus on what requires the most attention. If you feel flustered or burned-out, sit with yourself for a minute and figure out why. Maybe you've been home all week with the kids, and you feel claustrophobic. You may need some quiet time in nature. Maybe you had a relatively easy week with daily life, but you haven't been praying or going to the masjid. You may need spiritual rejuvenation. Maybe your irritability is due to a fight with a loved one, and you need to fix things.

Ask Yourself . . .

What do I need at this moment?

Are all parts of me in equilibrium and taken care of?

Being deeply connected with yourself helps you become self-aware, enabling you to practice self-care that benefits your entire being. With this understanding in mind, let's explore some specific ways you can enhance your self-care practices.

Self-Care for Your Heart

What is the most valuable thing we own? Is it the gold we've inherited? Our children? Our homes? In reality, our spiritual hearts are the most valuable things we could ever have. On the Day of Judgment, our hearts will be what Allah examines and judges. Nothing will benefit us more than a sound heart on that day.

> *Abu Salih reported that Abu Huraira (may Allah be pleased with him) said, "The heart is king, and its soldiers are the limbs. If the king is set right, his soldiers will be set right. If the king is corrupted, his soldiers will be corrupted." (* Shu'ab al-iman*)*

Because your heart rules over your actions, safeguarding your heart will affect other parts of you. Any religious practice that brings calmness to the heart and brings you closer to Allah ﷻ is heart self-care. Here are a few ideas:

1. **Do istighfar.** *Istighfar* is the simple yet powerful act of asking Allah ﷻ for forgiveness. It is often done by saying *"Astaghfirullah,"* which means "I seek forgiveness from Allah." *Istighfar* cleanses us spiritually, bringing us closer to Allah ﷻ and providing inner peace.

   Abu Huraira (may Allah be pleased with him) reported: The Messenger of Allah ﷺ said, "Verily, when the servant commits a sin, a black mark appears upon his heart. **If he abandons the sin, seeks forgiveness, and repents, then his heart will be polished.** If he returns to the sin, the blackness will be increased until it overcomes his heart. It is the covering that Allah has mentioned: 'No, rather a covering is over their hearts from what they have earned'" (*Shu'ab al-iman*). A clean heart is a cared-for heart.

2. *Make* **tahlil.** *Tahlil* is the practice of saying *"La ilaha illa Allah,"* which affirms there is no God worthy of worship except Allah ﷻ. It is an easy and powerful way of constantly renewing our faith in Allah; it doesn't even require moving our lips!

3. *Remember death.* On a random day, go and visit a cemetery (preferably a Muslim one, so that you can also make *du'a* for the deceased while there). A cemetery is a concrete representation of our inevitable next home and a reminder of this world's brevity. Visiting one is a solemn experience that has a powerful effect on the heart, evoking humility, reflection, and a renewed focus on what truly matters in life.

4. *Be mindful of your consumption.* Just as we wouldn't leave the doors and windows of our home wide open day and night, we must also guard the gateways to our hearts—the eyes and ears. Be discerning about what you allow into them. Be intentional about who you follow on social media and who you associate and spend time with in real life.

Self-Care for Your *Nafs*

In today's world, there is a strong emphasis on seeking maximum pleasure at any cost, often overshadowing the values of discipline, higher purpose, and a meaningful life. As Muslims, we are called to rise above this mindset. We are not meant to be gluttonous, consuming every pleasure in excess, since this can lead to the hardening of our hearts and the loss of meaning in our lives.

The *nafs* is the part of us that thrives on self-indulgence and excessive desires, which can distract us from our true purpose and cause us to become heedless of Allah ﷻ. Allah ﷻ has told us that the outcome of gaining control of our desires is nothing short of Paradise:

> *But as for him who feared standing before his Lord, and*
> *restrained himself from impure evil desires and lusts.*
> *Verily, Paradise will be his abode. (Qur'an 79:40–41)*

In the same way an invasive tumor can harm the host body, our *nafs* can damage our spiritual well-being. Thus, we must constantly be on guard to protect our spiritual hearts from the negative effects of the *nafs*. Here are two ways to help control the *nafs*:

1. **Fast.** One of the most powerful ways to control desires is through fasting. Fasting sharpens our awareness of our deeper needs and priorities by stripping away distractions. Experiencing physical hunger helps us reduce focus on trivial matters.

2. **Volunteer your time.** If your circumstances allow for it, volunteer your time to serve someone who is in more need

than you. If your kids are young, you don't even have to leave your home; you can offer to watch the children of someone who may be struggling more than you.

Self-Care for Your *'Aql* (Intelligence)

The average person today is bombarded with the equivalent of 174 newspapers of data a day! We are not capable of soaking up so much information while staying mentally and emotionally healthy. We need to limit the amount of information we take in in order to avoid information overload, burnout, and dopamine addiction. This might mean limiting social media or news and TV. The key is balance—consuming just enough to stay informed within a specific period during the day. There are other important ways to engage in intellectual self-care:

1. **Memorize Qur'an.** If you are a *hafidha* (someone who has memorized the Qur'an) or are already engaged in memorizing the Qur'an, review what you know. Learn other Qur'an-related skills, like studying the Arabic language or *tafseer* (the interpretation of the Qur'an). Remain consistent: It is not about becoming a full-time student of knowledge, but about dedicating consistent time to these wholesome pursuits. Just a small amount of time each day can lead to so much intellectual growth! Small but steady steps are especially practical for those who have other serious responsibilities, such as motherhood.

2. **Read.** Reading keeps those brain cells alive and strong. This is true even if you're only reading for fifteen minutes

a day, squeezing it in while the kids are playing at the park or while waiting at the doctor's office.

3. **Take a walk.** The stress hormone cortisol can destroy brain cells. Walking can reduce levels of this harmful hormone and cause the release of endorphins, or the "feel-good hormone." Studies show that cognitive abilities increase with just twenty minutes of walking! Make moving your body a regular part of self-care.

Self-Care for Your Body

Our body's *haqq* (right) over us demands that we give it what it needs. On the road to loving and healing ourselves, we need to care about ourselves enough to nourish the physical vessel that makes up our body. Part of being a Muslimah who chooses to live a life of excellence is developing our physical bodies and caring for our health. Here are some suggestions for how you can take better care of your physical self:

1. **Practice grooming.** The Prophet ﷺ took care of himself physically, as the many ahadith found in the *Shama'il* of al-Tirmidhi show us. He combed and oiled his hair regularly, made sure his clothing was clean and presentable, and generally always made sure he looked good. Put some effort into looking put together. You don't have to look glamorous, but do make an effort to put on clothes that are coordinated and make you look and feel good.

2. **Sleep.** Sleep is so important that it is even mentioned in the Qur'an as one sign that points to Allah's existence and power.

Among His signs are your sleep, by night and by day,
and your seeking His bounty. There truly are signs
in this for those who can hear. (Qur'an 30:23)

Sleep is not just a human need but a divine gift. When we neglect rest, we deny ourselves a form of Allah's mercy, one that underscores His wisdom in creating balance for all living things.

The Prophet ﷺ, our guide who didn't leave anything out, also emphasized the importance of sleep in many ahadith. This one beautifully illustrates the need to stop working ourselves to the point of exhaustion:

The Prophet ﷺ came into the mosque and noticed a rope stretched between two poles. He enquired, "What is this rope for?" He was told, "This is Zainab's rope. When during her voluntary prayer, she begins to feel tired, she grasps it for support." The Prophet ﷺ said, "Untie it. You should perform prayers so long as you feel active. When you feel tired, you should go to sleep." (Sahih al-Bukhari and Sahih Muslim)

The Prophet ﷺ was teaching us to listen to our bodies and give them a right to rest when necessary.

Sleep deprivation is disastrous. Recent science has discovered that our brain uses sleep time to flush out poisonous elements. If the cleanup process is constantly derailed because we don't get enough sleep, it will eventually impact our health.

3. **Eat a balanced diet.** We don't have to cook elaborate meals every day. A meal plan should reflect the philosophy of KISS!—Keep it simply sunnah. Bread with vinegar is

one food that is mentioned in the *Shama'il* of al-Tirmidhi, as are dates, watermelon, and other simple things. Choose uncomplicated, nutritious fare for the tough days: Our kids are more resilient than they look and they will happily take a simple meal with a rested mom over a tired and cranky mom with a full spread.

Self-Care for Your Libido

When intimacy between spouses is discussed, the focus is usually on ways to enhance it, obstacles that hinder it, and advice for those facing challenges with desire.

However, we don't hear enough about the other side of the coin. We don't hear about Muslims who struggle with sexual desires because they are not married. If we do, it is targeted to men—unmarried young men who are simply told to fast. It feels like no one thinks about women, when Allah ﷻ also created us with sexual desire. In fact, there are around 10,000 nerve endings on the clitoris, while the head of the penis only has around 4,000! Whether it is the innate modesty and shyness that Allah ﷻ has put in women or social norms and conditioning, we don't see many women being vocal about this topic.

We are created to be sexual and sensual beings. Even if we aren't being intimate, we do have desires—and we don't need to be ashamed of it. Since divorced women have experienced physical intimacy, they may struggle more than the proverbial young man who has no idea what intimacy is like.

I want to begin by saying that I see you. Allah ﷻ sees you. There you are, a beautiful woman, who quietly struggles and seeks to uphold Allah's command. You could potentially date multiple men or have one-night stands—both of which wider society supports—but you do not. You pray and keep yourself chaste. Never forget that al-Baseer (the All-Seeing) is rewarding you for your restraint. It is important to acknowledge and recognize that what you do for His sake is never ignored or forgotten.

Intimacy encompasses more than sexual connection; it also includes emotional, intellectual, and spiritual connections. While sexual relations in marriage often provide physical intimacy, emotional intimacy (feeling understood, loved, and supported) can be nurtured in many other ways. Meaningful nonsexual relationships can fulfill emotional intimacy needs, and having these connections in place makes it much easier to cope with the absence of physical intimacy.

Here are a few tips for managing your libido as a single woman:

1. **Make your struggle an act of 'ibadah (worship).** Whenever you miss intimacy, turn to Allah, and say, "Oh Allah, please count this as a rewardable action—reward me for my struggle and for my patience." Know that you are being rewarded by Allah for your struggle!

   Abu Qatadah reported: The Prophet ﷺ said, "Verily, you will never leave anything for the sake of Allah Almighty but that Allah will replace it with something better for you" (*Musnad Ahmad*).

   This hadith assures us that Allah sees and rewards every sacrifice we make for His sake. This isn't just about material replacement; it may also mean that Allah is deepening your inner strength, nurturing your contentment, or bringing you closer to Him as part of that "something better." So, when you endure, remember that your struggle creates space for divine mercy, growth, and unseen rewards, all fully known to Allah.

2. **Guard yourself online.** When using Muslim marriage apps, it's wise to opt for platforms that allow you to involve a *mahram* (a male guardian or family member) right from the start. This adds a layer of protection and accountability to your interactions. It's also crucial to understand the right way to court while following Islamic principles.

   Your gut feeling is your ally. If anything in your conversations or interactions doesn't sit right with you, it's essential not to brush it aside. End the conversation immediately and talk to your *mahram* about it later. It is also better to avoid using the apps at night—it can help save you from more doors for Shaytan, since people in general feel less inhibited at night.

3. **Know your cycle.** Track the changes in your body and how you feel at different times of the month, and you will see a pattern. Unless you're on birth control or some other types of medication, most women feel more aroused during their ovulation period. This is usually around fourteen days from the first day of your period. (If the first day of your period was February 1; you will ovulate around February 14.) At this time, there is a surge in the hormones that prime the body for conception. To increase the chances of conceiving, our body sends signals to make us desire to be intimate.

   You may also feel more aroused right before your period is about to start. The exact reason for this preperiod arousal is unknown, although there are theories. For our purposes, what we care about is nailing down your own personal pattern. Use a calendar for about three months to track the first and last day of your period. Mark the days you feel heightened arousal. At the end of the three months, identify the pattern. Plan ahead: Fast on these days or fill your schedule with meaningful activities.

The Prophet ﷺ provided us with fasting as a shield to protect ourselves because he understood the intensity of desires. "Fasting is a shield; it will protect you from the fire and prevent you from committing sins" (*Sahih al-Bukhari*). He ﷺ guided us toward a means that enhances our ability to channel and control these desires, transforming a natural urge into a rewardable act of worship.

4. **Seek out emotional connection.** Think of a friend or family member who can offer support. Call them ahead of time and plan to visit around ovulation or period days. Build deep, nurturing relationships with friends and other family that bring genuine connection. If you feel like you are a lone bird and struggle with making friends, see the Additional Resources section in the back of this book. There are resources to help you. For now, know that it is within your reach to have a thriving friendship life. With a bit of intentional effort, you can build a meaningful support network.

5. **Think about your purpose.** What do you feel called to do in service of others? Revisit the discussion on purpose in Chapter 4. Channel your energy toward something you love, and derive connection and emotional intimacy from

those spaces. This is a fulfilling way to divert focus from sexual urges and serves as a powerful way to express emotions and energy.

Remember, you can't give what you don't have. Self-care isn't indulgent; it's essential for thriving. It's a crucial ingredient in becoming the woman you aspire to be and the mother your children need. Self-care lays the groundwork for your new life ahead. In the next chapter, we'll explore the realities and challenges of parenting without a partner.

CHALLENGE

Your challenge for this chapter is to discover ways to nurture your whole self. By attending to your physical, mental, emotional, and spiritual needs, you'll create a foundation that allows you to thrive in your new postdivorce life.

1. What self-care practice will you adopt for each aspect of your being?

   Heart Care:

   Nafs Care:

   'Aql Care:

   Body Care:

Tracking your period

1. When was the first day of your period this month?

2. Count fourteen days from the date you noted above. This is your estimated ovulation time. Note the date.

3. Make an intention to fast on your days of ovulation, and plan for it practically.

4. Are there other days that you notice feeling sexually aroused? This commonly occurs a few days before a cycle of bleeding begins.

5. Repeat this pattern recognition exercise for three months. What patterns have emerged? How can you now take preemptive measures for your chastity and spiritual well-being during these times?

6. List the two or three family members or friends you will reach out to for emotional intimacy.

12

Parenting Solo

Hajar (peace be upon her) stood alone in the vast desert with her infant son, surrounded by nothing but endless sand and silence. Prophet Ibrahim (peace be upon him), following Allah's command, had left them in a place with no water, no food, and no one else nearby. Confused and scared, Hajar called out to Ibrahim as he walked away, "Are you really leaving us here?" He didn't reply. Desperate for understanding, she asked again, "Is this something Allah has commanded you to do?" Ibrahim turned and nodded silently. In that moment, her fear shifted to trust. "Then we will be OK," she said, placing her full reliance on Allah to take care of her and her child.

When talks of divorce began just three months after my daughter's birth, strangely enough, one of the most dominant thoughts I had was, "Who will teach her to ride a bike? Her father lives in another state!" Of all the issues I could have worried about, somehow the idea of the bike consumed me. I grappled with a deep sense of guilt for marrying someone who would become an ex. The challenges of single parenting constantly felt like a punishment for what I saw as my "mistake." I couldn't believe we were about to become a statistic—that of a broken home.

However, I had forgotten something important. I had forgotten that I am merely human and powerless to control the outcomes of things. Was I supposed to predict the future?

If this is you now, make some room for Allah's plans, please! Allah in His wisdom chose our children's fathers; perhaps their destiny is to not have their father actively in their lives. Or maybe that will change. Allah knows best. He alone knows the future. What is within your power in the present moment? What can *you* change? Imagine if your kids have an emotionally intelligent, grounded, full of faith, serene, and content mother who navigates life with grace, *tawakkul*, and *iman*. Single mom or otherwise, this is the best gift that we can give our children. They will be secure, confident people because of the work we do on ourselves.

Everything is not as it seems on the surface. Allah ﷻ has told us that He is the best of planners, and that means we are not! Even though my child's father is not close to her, I know that it is still the best thing for her—because Allah chose it. Whether I come to understand the wisdom in this world or only in the hereafter, that knowledge rests with Allah. However, acknowledging that there is indeed a wisdom behind what Allah ﷻ decrees brings me a sense of peace.

Trusting in Allah's knowledge and acknowledging our own limited information is part of our belief in *qadr*. With this *tawakkul* in our hearts, let us delve into some day-to-day struggles of being a single mother.

All moms have it hard, but not having a spouse to hand your child to so that you can take a break is one of a single mother's unique challenges. Even when emotions hit hard and threaten to take you out, you are the only parent available to your child. The upcoming sections explain how to work through some common emotions.

Frustration and Anger

There are many factors that contribute to making us frustrated and angry. While emotions are natural, examining our triggers is imperative. Sometimes, we are just tired and haven't had a chance to do things that make us happy, like enjoy a hobby or see friends. Other times, our frustration is due to financial hardship, not getting enough sleep, or decision-making fatigue. Whatever it may be, we need to figure it out, then address the root problem. We need to be in tune with our internal world, so that we can recognize when we are about to reach our limit.

We are, of course, only human. We will inevitably stumble, snap, and overreact when we are worn thin. However, when these mistakes happen, we need to apologize and hold ourselves accountable. Even these moments are opportunities to model good character to our children.

If you struggle with perpetual rage, more work may be needed to get to the root cause of your anger. The rage is the tip of the iceberg, and an exploration of the pain underneath may be necessary. Understanding ourselves intimately—our triggers, fears, and underlying worries—helps us navigate these moments of anger with greater clarity. After all, true strength lies not in force, but in restraint. As the Prophet ﷺ said, "The strong one is the one who can control himself in the time of anger," reminding us that inner mastery, especially in moments of anger, is a true mark of strength (*Sahih al-Bukhari*).

Try this exercise. Before entering your child's presence, take a few moments to close your eyes and visualize this: You are carrying bags of groceries, trying to balance them all. They are heavy, and you have at least three bags in each hand. It makes you a little wobbly under the weight. Slowly, you walk toward a storage shed by the door, open it, and put the bags down. Phew! What a relief. That is your anger, your frustration, your mental load, your emotional baggage. You can pick it up later; it is not going anywhere. Having lightened your load, go be present with your child.

Anxiety About the Future

As if there wasn't enough to worry about in the present, we often can't stop ourselves from worrying about the future. I spent so many days and nights engulfed in anxiety about my daughter's future emotional and psychological well-being. Will she grow up to have "daddy issues"? Will she be less confident because her dad is not present? Will she feel bad at school when seeing other kids with their dads?

This thought process has a problematic underlying assumption— that I am somehow in control of her future or know what will unfold. In reality, I may end up dead tomorrow, and she may go to her father full-time! When Musa's mother put her son in a box and put him on the river, she had no idea what would happen next. She trusted her *rabb* (Lord) fully.

When overwhelm takes over, remember that no one knows the future. When anxiety creeps in, recite *"La hawla wa la quwwata illa billah"* ("There is no power and no strength except with Allah"). Repeat it until its meaning anchors in your heart. Focus on strengthening your mental well-being and becoming a steady, faithful mom, and leave the rest to Allah. If you are present and in tune with what is happening here and now, you will be able to recognize and address any emotional or psychological challenges if and when they arise.

Financial Fears

A powerful story from the life of Hasan al-Basri (may Allah have mercy on him) highlights the incredible, transformative power of *istighfar*. Once, three people came to Hasan al-Basri, each burdened by a unique hardship. One struggled with poverty, another was desperate for rain to save his crops, and the third was heartbroken over the lack of children in his life. To each, Hasan al-Basri offered the same advice: make abundant *istighfar*—seek forgiveness from Allah.

When questioned about why he gave the same answer to three unique questions, Hasan al-Basri explained that Prophet Nuh (peace be upon him) told his people about the many blessings of *istighfar*:

> *I said, "Ask forgiveness of your Lord: He is ever forgiving.*
> *He will send down abundant rain from the sky for*
> *you; He will give you wealth and sons; He will provide*
> *you with gardens and rivers. (Qur'an 71:10–12)*

The Prophet Muhammad ﷺ also emphasized the power of *istigfar* when he said,

> *If anyone continually asks pardon, Allah will appoint*
> *for them a way out of every distress, a relief from*
> *every anxiety, and will provide for them from where*
> *they cannot imagine. (*Sunan Abu Dawud*)*

These verses and ahadith teach us that *istighfar* is not only a plea for forgiveness—it's a powerful means of inviting Allah's provision, including financial blessings. **It is a means of Allah ﷺ showering us with provisions we never saw coming!**

When we turn to Allah with sincerity, He doesn't just erase our sins; He opens unexpected avenues of sustenance and wealth. Through *istighfar*, the financial hardships that once seemed insurmountable can become moments of ease, as Allah provides in ways we could never foresee, bringing relief, prosperity, and blessings beyond what we had imagined.

Make an active decision to do *istighfar* regularly. Plan out when you will make it a part of your day—after salah, while driving to work, or before bed. Speak your intentions aloud right now: "I will make *istighfar* while I am on my way to work." We tend to commit more to things we say aloud than those we merely think of in our head.

Barakah (blessing) is such an overlooked but important factor when it comes to our provision. There have been many times when I thought I had only $200 or so in my account and expected my card to be declined, but it wasn't, store after store. I have also experienced the reverse: a large amount decreasing rapidly with not much to show for it. It truly is more about quality than quantity.

The concept of *barakah* is real and we have all experienced it in one form or another.

The Prophet's *du'a* after he completed Fajr prayer was, "Oh Allah, I ask You for knowledge which is beneficial and **sustenance which is good**, and deeds which are accepted" (*Sunan Ibn Majah*). Make this dua constantly to place *barakah* into the *rizq* you already have as well.

Time Management

There just doesn't seem to be enough time to do everything I need to do in a day. Not only do I have to make sure my daughter's meals are made, but I have to make sure she eats them too. From ensuring her hair and nails are clean to managing laundry, maintaining social activities, researching schools, making decisions about upcoming engagements, keeping track of doctors' appointments, and handling my job, it feels like the responsibilities are endless. It is one task after another, and there just isn't enough time in the day.

Yet we hear stories of people of the past who accomplished so much more. Ibn Rushd, a twelfth-century Andalusian scholar, wrote commentaries on almost all of Aristotle's work, as well as books on medicine, philosophy, and *fiqh* (the rules of Islamic law). In addition, he was married and had a full-time career as a *qadi* (judge). Imam Nawawi did not live past the age of forty, but he wrote at least fifty books!

Whereas for us, time seems to have shrunk. Everyone has noticed this, not just single moms. The truth is that time has indeed been changing since the era of our predecessors!

Anas ibn Malik reported that the Messenger of Allah ﷺ said, "The Hour will not be established until time passes rapidly, such that a year is like a month, a month is like a week, a week is like a day, a day is like an hour, and an hour is like the flicker of a flame" (*Jami' al-Tirmidhi*).

However, we can still take some measures to have *barakah* in our time and accomplish our responsibilities as well as goals.

Practical Tips for Barakah in Your Time

1. **Guard your sleep.** Go to bed as soon as you pray 'Isha and wake up early for Fajr. Our bodies are made to follow the rhythm of nature, to rise with the sun and sleep at its setting. With technology that provides limitless artificial light, we have been staying up longer and longer. How many of us really wake up refreshed and rested in the morning? So many mornings feel like an extension of the night before, due to our disturbed circadian rhythms. Johann Hariri mentions in his book, *Stolen Focus: Why You Can't Pay Attention—and How to Think Deeply Again*, "The less you sleep, the more the world blurs in every way—in your immediate focus, in your ability to think deeply and make connections, and in your memory."

   When we sleep, our brain cleans itself of waste and toxic substances. There is a sophisticated system called the glymphatic system that accomplishes the task of "rinsing" our brains, mostly when we are asleep. The fogginess of sleep deprivation is partially because our brain hasn't had the chance to finish the cleanup process! If we don't go to sleep early and wake up refreshed, we won't be able to reap the benefits of *barakah* that Allah ﷻ put in the Fajr hours.

2. **Cut down on digital time.** Most of us struggle with the time we spend on social media—it's a major time suck that often leaves us feeling guilty. Other forms of digital technology, like email and texting, can be equally distracting and time-consuming. The issue with time lost to phones and social media is that it's not just the few minutes we spend "quickly" checking Twitter that vanish; at least another twenty-five minutes are consumed as we try to regain our focus on the task at hand. If we check our phone for a few minutes every hour and factor in the twenty-five-minute refocusing period, we end up spending our entire day in fractured increments, depleting its *barakah*.

   However, for the change to be effective, we need to make sure the time we would have spent digitally is replaced with a meaningful activity. If you haven't done so already, go to the purpose chapter and do the exercise to find a meaningful activity you can include in your life.

3. **Read the Qur'an.** The Qur'an is prescribed for its many benefits, including increasing *barakah* in one's time. However, because we hear this advice repeatedly, we end up ignoring it—even though we know it's correct! It's a bit like being told to eat clean to lose weight; everyone knows that it works, but most people don't follow through.

   I wrote this chapter on a day I had read some Qur'an. After reading a few verses of the Qur'an, I made two stews, washed clothes, worked on this chapter, and took care of my daughter. Those few minutes with the Qur'an blessed my entire day. A small dose of remembering Allah can fuel immense productivity. The reason we hear the same advice repeated time and again is simple—it works!

4. **Give *sadaqah* with your time.** Allah ﷻ promises to multiply and return whatever we spend for His sake: "Charitable men and women who make a good loan to God will have it doubled and receive a generous reward" (Qur'an 57:18). When we use our time with the intention of pleasing Him, He blesses it with extra *barakah*. We'll find that we have time not only for good deeds but also for additional activities we didn't expect. So dedicate some time for His pleasure, knowing He will repay it with abundant reward.

5. **Be grateful.** Allah has told us that if we are grateful, He will give us even more (Qur'an 14:7). Practicing gratitude improves all areas of our life, including time management. Be grateful for whatever time you already have!

Your Superpower: *Du'a*

In the time of the Prophet ﷺ, a *sahaba* (companion) was riding a camel when it sat down and wouldn't get up. The man then said, in the presence of the Prophet ﷺ, "Get up! May Allah curse you!" The Prophet ﷺ said, "Get off your camel, and do not ride with us on an animal you have cursed." Then the Prophet ﷺ continued, "Do not make *du'a* against yourself, your wealth, or your family. For it may be that your *du'a* will happen at a time when Allah answers all *du'a*, and you will not want that" (*Sahih Muslim*).

In one of his Visionaire program sessions, Shaykh Muhammad Al-Shareef (may Allah have mercy on him) shared a story about a mother and her teenage son. The boy was at an age when kids are eager to drive, and he would pester and nag his mother for the car all the time. One day, she got tired of his nagging, so she handed him the keys in frustration and said, "Here you go! May you never come back!"

What do you think happened next? If you guessed that he didn't come back, you are right. The next person to knock on her door was a policeman, telling her about the passing of her son in an accident.

How did this story make you feel? Did your heart clench and your eyes tear up for the mom? Did you vow to never say anything bad in moments of anger and frustration? Good. That means you believe in the incredible power of your *du'a*. If you think making bad *du'a* is scary and its effects can touch your child, what about good *du'a*?

Du'a is a superpower we all have that needs to be utilized effectively. The Creator of all the worlds can do anything. Often, we hesitate to make sincere *du'a* because, deep down, we don't think it will actually work. It's as if we believe envisioning a process for it is a necessary precondition for the dua to come true. Subconsciously, we are thinking that if we don't know *how* something could happen, this must mean that it *can't* happen. Shaykh Muhammad said it best: "Don't put your limitations on Allah. It is not you answering you; it is Allah ﷻ responding to you."

Allah ﷻ loves to hear your prayer and responds to those who call upon Him. As He promises in the Qur'an, "Pray to Me, and I will respond to you" (Qur'an 40:60). The Prophet ﷺ

described the generosity of Allah: "Indeed, Allah is *hayy* [conscientious] and *kareem* [generous]: When a person raises their hands to Him, He feels too shy to return them empty and rejected" (*Jami' al-Tirmidhi*).

Dear sister, what are your hopes for your children? Each child is different and has different needs, so what is that one thing you want for each of them? Put this book down right now, raise your hands, and make *du'a* for your child. Make a designated time to make *du'a* every day for a few minutes. Consider making *du'a* after Fajr prayer a regular practice, or choose any other time you feel is going to help you stay consistent. Although special times like after 'Asr, during Ramadan, and during Dhul Hijjah are significant, we need regular, consistent *du'a* habits throughout the year as well. Hence, it is a good idea to also pick your own time to help you with consistency.

Solo parenting is filled with moments of deep uncertainty and fear. Raising children without a partner can feel isolating, but just like Hajar, we can find strength in relying on something greater than ourselves, knowing that through the struggle, we are never truly alone.

CHALLENGE

In this chapter, your challenge is to identify and implement effective strategies for managing the demands of parenting without a partner's support.

1. Identify some of your daily frustrations.

2. What is one thing you can do to address the root causes of these frustrations?

3. Which healthy coping mechanisms can you use to manage anger and frustration?

4. How can you ease anxiety about the future?

5. What practical steps can help you handle financial worries more effectively?

6. What changes will you make to bring more *barakah* into your time?

7. Name one consistent *du'a* you want to make for your family, and decide when you'll start.

13

Housekeeping Solo

The hum of the dishwasher fills the kitchen. You wipe down the counter and then give the pot a stir between quick glances at the clock. A child tugs at your leg, asking about homework, and in the back of your mind, tomorrow's errands are already taking shape. In the world of single parenthood, the art of housekeeping is unique, especially in the West. Our role as both solo caregiver and homemaker means we're constantly juggling the everyday demands of chores while ensuring the well-being of our children. For us, housekeeping is less about routine and more like a high-wire act—a neverending balancing act.

But there's a hidden beauty in this balancing act. With no one else to lean on, every chore can become more than just a task—it's a chance to set our intentions, ground ourselves, and turn the mundane into something deeper. In this chapter, we'll explore practical ways to manage a household solo, while bringing meaning and purpose to each step.

Practical Tips for Managing a Household Solo

As we dive into these tips, think of each one as an opportunity to approach the practical demands of single parenthood with a renewed sense of purpose. These strategies aren't just about getting through the chores; they're about creating a home that reflects your values, your faith, and the love you pour into each day.

Set Your Intentions (Niyyah)

A beautiful part of our *deen* is that every action is judged by its intention, so do not forget to set your intentions for household tasks. Purifying your *niyyah* for even these mundane actions can lead to so many rewards! Before bed, the *sahaba* would intend to sleep so their bodies could rest and be refreshed for worshipping Allah ﷻ in the morning.

Remember to make the intention for *'ibadah* for everything you do. For example, I am cooking this soup to provide a healthy, nutritious meal for my children who are an *amanah* from you, Allah. Please count this as an act of worship.

Oh Allah, I am going to put the baby to bed and tucking him in so that I fulfill the *amanah* you gave me to look after this beautiful child.

Oh Allah, I am throwing out this bag of trash to keep a clean home for Your sake and to take care of the home you have provided for me.

Your intentions do not have to turn into long monologues; just remember to maintain the conscious reminder in your heart that "Allah, I'm doing this for your sake!" Inshallah, by establishing this intention for worship, your everyday tasks will be counted as significant good deeds in the sight of Allah.

Setting a *niyyah* for every task requires us to slow down, be intentional, and focus on what we are doing. In today's fast-paced world, being constantly on the move is often seen as praiseworthy. As a result, we find it hard to pause, make our intentions, and be present in our activities.

We have a limited cognitive capacity and are inherently single-minded. Yet, instead of recognizing these human limits, we've created a myth—that we can think about multiple things simultaneously. In truth, we're just rapidly shifting from one task to another.

Focusing on one task at a time will not only give you a chance to set intentions, it will also contribute to your cognitive health. Focus on each task as you do it.

Once you have identified what tasks need to be completed in a day, just get them done. Don't overthink the nature of the tasks, when you'll do them, or how to do them. Some mornings, I catch myself thinking anxiously about the day ahead. "OK, once I'm done with my shower, I must get started on lunch. Oh, good thing I still have some tomato sauce left. Then I will take care of Dhuhr and go pick up my girl. Hmm, I wonder if it's better to grab the meds on the way back home, or should I just do it after five o'clock?"

This type of mental dialogue will exhaust you before you even get started with your tasks. Mental fatigue is sometimes worse than physical tiredness.

Prioritize Your Pet Peeves

Before tackling your chores, figure out your pet peeve: What is the one task that will leave you unbearably irritated if it doesn't get done? Prioritize this task and put it at the top of your list! That way, if you don't get anything else done that day, at least your main pet peeve is out of the way. If your pet peeve is undone and you have kids who still nap, let's face it—you won't be napping with them. The reality is that the house is waiting for you. If your child wakes up, what is one thing you will regret not doing? Start with that.

My pet peeve is having a cluttered floor. The sight of toys and dust on my hardwood floor really bothers me, so I make sure to clean that first. Dirty dishes don't bug me as much; I might be able to get to them while my daughter is playing. It might be different for you!

Let Go of Perfectionism

Perfectionism is the relentless pursuit of an ideal standard. In the context of household management, it is an unwavering focus on ensuring that everything—from cleanliness and organization to meal planning and time management—is executed flawlessly. This mindset often leads to setting unrealistic expectations for yourself, resulting in constant stress and a sense of inadequacy when those high standards are inevitably unmet.

This is not a healthy mindset or way of being, and it can make daily tasks feel overwhelming and diminish the joy of home life. We need to let go of our attachment to how we *wish* things were. The reality is that things will not always be the way we want them to be or the way they were while we were married or before we had a child. You are now a one-woman show with children who need you. Figure out your nonnegotiables: Is it a homemade lunch? Clean floors? An empty sink? Then turn a happy and carefree blind eye to the negotiables.

The objective of chores is to nurture the family. And there are certain things that must be prioritized in order to make sure the children grow up feeling safe, secure, and loved. But try to have a future-centered outlook and consider which chores will make you feel like you have achieved this. Then be OK with not doing the rest.

Minimize Clutter

Our home is supposed to be a sanctuary from the chaos of the outside world. Home is meant to be a "happy place," a place of comfort and tranquility. Filling a space beyond its capacity and letting it get disorganized will only lead to the drudgery of increased cleanup times and the frustration of searching for lost items. A recent study showed that clutter can affect mental health, leading to unhealthy eating, low subjective well-being, and less efficient thinking! Our role model the Messenger of Allah ﷺ lived a simple life. Numerous narrations paint a picture of a humble man living with the barest necessities. Umar ibn al-Khattab (may Allah be pleased with him) said:

> *I entered upon the Messenger of Allah ﷺ when he was*
> *[sitting] on a reed mat. I sat down and saw that he was*
> *wearing a waist wrap, and there was no other barrier*
> *between him and the mat but his waist wrap, and the reed*
> *mat had made marks on his side. And I saw a handful*

> *of barley, nearly a* sa' *[a small measure], and some acacia*
> *leaves, in a corner of the room, and a skin hanging up. My*
> *eyes flowed with tears, and he said: "Why are you weeping,*
> *Oh son of Khattab?" I said: "Oh Prophet of Allah, why*
> *should I not weep? This mat has made marks on your side,*
> *and this is all you have accumulated, I cannot see anything*
> *other than what I see [here], while Chosroes and Caesar live*
> *among fruits and rivers. You are the Prophet of Allah and*
> *His Chosen One, and this is what you have accumulated."*
> *He said: "Oh son of Khattab, does it not please you [to*
> *know] that [these things] are for us in the hereafter and for*
> *them in this world?" I said: "Yes." (*Sunan Ibn Majah*)*

The Prophet ﷺ has promised us unimaginable rewards in Jannah, including all we desire for our homes there.

In this life, create a peaceful, simple space free of clutter—one that's easy to care for and enjoy. Our physical environment affects our internal state—a cluttered house means a cluttered mind and heart. After tidying up a messy home, don't you feel so much better physically and emotionally? Avoid accumulating objects, purge as much as possible, and don't buy anything you don't need.

The Diderot effect. We often fall prey to accumulating too many toys, clothes, housewares, and everything in between. As a single mom, it's necessary to take a step back and reevaluate whether you *really* need that next purchase or not. The Diderot effect describes the tendency for a single purchase to lead to further buying, often because the new item makes what you already have seem insufficient or out of place. This creates a chain reaction of buying related or complementary items.

For example, you buy a new kitchen table, thinking it's a simple refresh. But when it arrives, you realize the old chairs don't fit the new table's height, so you buy a new set of chairs. Next, the chairs scrape against the floor, prompting you to purchase floor protectors or a rug. Then, you notice the placemats and tableware clash with the look of the new table, leading you to buy new dishes, utensils, and a table runner. What started as a table replacement quickly snowballs into a series of related (and possibly expensive!) purchases just to make the setup feel functional and cohesive.

Don't buy anything new without thoroughly thinking it through to ensure it's absolutely essential.

Get Efficient

Companies invest thousands of dollars into figuring out ways to make their businesses more efficient. They know that if they can decrease their production line's time by even two seconds, they will save thousands of dollars over the course of the year.

We need to apply this mindset to our homes as well—especially the kitchen! For example, is your salt behind a spice bottle that you barely use? Do you have to hunt for the oil, even though you need to use it every day? This may sound silly; after all, it barely takes a second to grab it. Nonetheless, it adds a subtle level of inconvenience and inefficiency to your day. If there are several spots like that in your house, all those extra seconds add up to wasted minutes and hours and contribute to an increasing sense of frustration.

Like a tightly run production line in a factory, your entire home needs to be rearranged to promote efficiency. Declutter first! Then look into a system of efficiency that works for you and your family. Arrange everything in a way that makes you move as effortlessly as possible. My spices are arranged in a row according to what I use the most. Spoons are not arranged by size, but by frequency of use and how easily I can grab them. There are many different resources for home organization and productivity online and offline—perhaps take the time to study them a little to figure out what works best for you.

Make Dhikr

Women's struggles with housework are a tale as old as time. Fatima (may Allah be pleased with her) was the daughter of the Prophet ﷺ. She was a woman who had perfected her faith, and she is the leader of the women of Paradise. She was also very much a real woman, as real as you and I. Fatima ran her own household, with two young children, and was exhausted by her duties. There were days when her hands cracked and bled from the physical labor she had to perform.

One day, hearing that the Muslims had acquired some slaves as part of their war booty, she went to her father to ask for a helper. The Prophet ﷺ could have easily given her the maid she wanted. After all, this was his beloved daughter. There was nothing in his power he would not do to alleviate her pain. Instead, the Prophet ﷺ offered an alternative solution. He advised her to recite specific praises of Allah before sleep: "Allahu akbar" (Allah is greater) thirty-four times, "*alhamdulillah*" (all praise is for Allah) thirty-three times, and "*subhanallah*" (glorified be Allah) thirty-three times. This, he told her, was better than any servant (*Sahih al-Bukhari* and *Sahih Muslim*).

Rather than providing his daughter with much-needed domestic help, the Prophet ﷺ instructed her to perform *dhikr* at night. I do not know if Fatima felt incredulous at that moment; I know I did when I first heard the hadith. Fatima was a righteous woman, and the Prophet ﷺ knew she would be able to use *dhikr* to help her through her difficulties. For the rest of us, who may not share that same level of faith, we may prefer to rely on tangible, practical means—like hiring help—to ease the burden, which is perfectly acceptable. But why not strive for a higher, spiritual means and follow Fatima's example? *Dhikr* develops closeness to Allah ﷻ. Allah tells us "And the men and the women who remember Allah much with their hearts and tongues Allah has prepared for them **forgiveness and a great reward** [i.e., Paradise]" (Qur'an 33:35).

The benefits of *dhikr* do not immediately result in a clean home or cooked meal. Rather, one of the benefits of regular *dhikr* is experiencing *barakah* in our life (which helps us in unexpected ways) and developing tranquility in our hearts.

The beautiful thing about *dhikr* is that it requires no preparation. There is no particular state we need to be in since remembering Allah is for all times and all states. You don't need to go out of your way to do *wudu* (ablution) to do *dhikr*; you don't have to be sitting down or facing the *qibla* (direction of prayer). All you need to do is recite the words with a conscious heart!

My favorite *dhikr* when working is "*la ilaha illa Allah*" because it is the easiest of all forms of *dhikr* to recite. It takes minimal effort and energy; the tongue moves while the lips stay still.

Housekeeping, when approached from the right perspective, can transform mundane chores into meaningful acts of worship. As single mothers, the weight of responsibility can often feel overwhelming, but remember that every task, no matter how small it is, can be an opportunity to seek the pleasure of Allah ﷻ. By using practical strategies and incorporating spiritual practices into your routine, you can create a sanctuary of faith and tranquility for both yourself and your children.

It is also reassuring to know that many women before you have navigated this path and found success. Their experiences offer valuable lessons and inspiration. In the next chapter, we will explore the stories of these remarkable women, whose journeys can provide practical guidance and encouragement as you continue your own.

CHALLENGE

Your challenge for this chapter is to transform your home into a nurturing environment that supports you and your family. Dive into the practical and spiritual tips provided to create a space filled with warmth, comfort, and love. Take time to reflect on what a nurturing home means to you, and identify specific actions you can implement—whether it's decluttering, establishing routines, or adding spiritual practices.

1. What can help you consistently remember to set intentions for '*ibadah* when doing your chores?

2. Which area of your home would benefit most from decluttering?

Declutter checklist
- Start with a small area (drawer, shelf, closet).
- Remove duplicates (keep only what's necessary).
- Toss expired food, medicine, and beauty products.
- Sort and keep only essential paperwork.
- Store items in labeled containers or bins.
- Empty and organize your purse (remove receipts, trash, and nonessentials).
- Keep books you truly love or reference often, and donate the rest.

3. What steps can you take to improve the efficiency of your home's setup?

4. What *dhikr* will you engage in while performing your chores?

5. Which household chores will make you feel like you have nurtured your family?

6. Which chores are nice-to-haves, or the ones you can let go of?

14

Inspiring Trailblazers

John Elton Bembry was born in 1912 in Edenton, North Carolina. He grew up during the Great Depression, a time of economic hardship in the US. Although he started life in a loving and stable family, a series of family tragedies left him alone and poor at a young age. Forced into a life of crime, partly due to systemic racism in the segregated South, he soon became prisoner #22138. However, his story doesn't end there.

Much of the current Islamic presence in America owes a debt to Bembry. Whether through African Americans who embraced Islam or immigrants who benefit from the struggles of their African American predecessors, Bembry's impact is profound yet often overlooked. His most influential mentee in prison was Malcolm X, who described him as "the first man I had ever seen command total respect . . . with his words." Malcolm X began learning from Bembry, or "Bimby," as he called him. Malcolm would later embrace mainstream Islam, teach thousands of others, and become a pivotal figure in the civil rights movement.

John Elton Bembry's influence on Malcolm X demonstrates the impact of powerful role models. The influence of a single person can change history. As the Messenger of Allah ﷺ told us, the company we keep will be reflected in our own character—either for better or for worse.

Abu Musa (may Allah be pleased with him) reported that the Prophet ﷺ said, "Verily, the parable of good company and bad company is only that of a seller of musk and a blacksmith. The seller of musk will give you some perfume, you will buy some, or you will notice a good smell. As for the blacksmith, he will burn your clothes or you will notice a bad smell" (*Sahih al-Bukhari* and *Sahih Muslim*).

In other words, to embody a certain characteristic or way of being, it is necessary to surround yourself with people who are modeling that behavior.

In the journey of raising Muslim children as divorced parents, finding role models to learn from is nonnegotiable. There are a plethora of people we can use as role models, whether from the past or from current times, from a distance or from right in front of us. There are so many women in our own communities who show us what it means to raise Allah-loving children. These women have faced adversity with bravery, faith, and certainty in Allah ﷺ. Their stories can give us hope, strength, and powerful lessons to apply to our own lives.

As mothers, our number one goal for our kids is to be dwellers of Jannah. The mothers below had a vision, and they consistently worked on that vision with *tawakkul*. We can do the same!

Rumaysa bint Milhan (Umm Sulaym)

Rumaysa (may Allah be pleased with her) embraced Islam even before the Prophet ﷺ migrated to Medina. At the time, her husband, who was frequently away on business trips, was absent. Upon his return, he was infuriated by her conversion. Despite his anger, Rumaysa continued to teach their young child to recite *"La ilaha illa Allah,"* which only aggravated him further. He would accuse her of corrupting their son. Eventually, her husband left again and later died, leaving Rumaysa alone with their child. She realized that she had no choice but to rise to the challenge of raising a Jannah-dweller alone. However, Rumaysa realized that her son needed a positive male role model in his life. She wasn't shy about asking for help—and so she picked the best man she knew. She entrusted her son to the care and guidance of the Prophet ﷺ. This son was none other than Anas ibn Malik (may Allah be pleased with him), who became one of the greatest companions of the Prophet ﷺ and an amazing scholar of Islam.

Having a positive masculine role model is crucial. If your ex-husband is not positively and sufficiently involved in your children's lives, it is important to find a family or community member who can serve as a mentor. You must proactively reach out, express your need for their involvement, and be open about your desire for them to play an active role in your children's lives. If close family members are unavailable, seeking out a trustworthy couple and explaining the situation is essential. Devout Muslims who share your spiritual and personal values are likely to understand and embrace the broader vision you aim to achieve.

Sitt al-Rakb (Ibn Hajar al-Asqalani's sister)

The great scholar Ibn Hajar al-Asqalani lost both his parents when he was less than five years old. His sister, Sitt al-Rakb, rose to the occasion, raising her younger brother to become the great Hafiz Ibn Hajar al-Asqalani. By the age of twelve, he was leading *tarawih* salah in Masjid al-Haram. Hafiz Ibn Hajar al-Asqalani's intellect is a thing of legend among hadith scholars. His sister and his uncle's wife were instrumental in shaping the man and scholar he later became.

Ramla bint Abu Sufyan (Umm Habiba)

Umm Habiba (may Allah be pleased with her) was another female companion of the Prophet ﷺ who demonstrated strength and resilience in times of difficulty. After embracing Islam, Umm Habiba left the home she had always known and migrated with a small group of other Muslims to Abyssinia in order to avoid persecution. Soon after they reached Abyssinia, her husband died, leaving her with their young daughter.

Although Umm Habiba had a wealthy father she could have gone back home to, she stood her ground and raised her daughter with Islam. In a faraway land with very few other Muslims around her, Umm Habiba was committed to ensuring that her daughter's heart was filled with the love of Allah ﷻ and His Messenger ﷺ. After many years, Allah ﷻ rewarded her patience and strength with a marriage to the Prophet ﷺ.

The Mothers of the Giants

Of those individuals in Islamic history whose legacies are so remarkable that they are remembered and referenced daily worldwide, many of them, including Imam Bukhari, Imam Shafi'i, Imam Ahmed, and Imam Malik, were all raised by single mothers. It is reported that Imam Ahmed said:

> *My mother helped me to memorize the Qur'an when I was a boy of just ten years of age. She would wake me up before the time of the Fajr prayer and warm the water for me to take wudu, during the cold nights in Baghdad. She would dress me up and then cover herself with her hijab and accompany me to the masjid, due to the distance of our house from the masjid and the darkness of the night.*

If these mothers were visionaries who were determined to make something out of their kids, and they made *du'a* to Allah and He answered them, why can't you and I do the same? They did not just worry about work or their provision. Their visions for their children were lofty; they had big goals and dreams. Ultimately, our job is to raise the children Allah entrusted to us with *ihsan* (excellence), to raise children who know and submit to their Lord.

Studying these exemplary figures from Islamic history provides us with invaluable guidance. We can look to them as models for our own lives, striving to emulate their virtues and achievements. However, their stories also show us the importance of finding contemporary role models and communities we can be a part of. Our children are a sacred trust, and by surrounding them with positive influences, we honor our roles as both believers and mothers.

CHALLENGE

Your challenge for this chapter is to intentionally recognize role models who empower you. This will enhance the quality of your life, because it will help you draw strength and support needed for your journey.

1. Who is a role model mother in your local community to whom you can reach out to for guidance and support?

2. How can you enhance the environment that you and your children are exposed to?

3. What is one thing you can do to cultivate meaningful relationships with other women in your community?

4. What activities or groups can you join to meet other families and build connections?

CONCLUSION

Navigating the complexities of divorce is undeniably challenging and painful, but it also offers an opportunity for life-changing growth. I hope that as you have journeyed through the pages of this book, you have gained insights, strategies, and tools to help you heal, rebuild, and thrive postdivorce.

You are a magnificent creation of Allah ﷻ, with divine worth and purpose. Divorce was in your *qadr*, along with the lessons and growth it brings with it.

Your quest, should you accept it, asks you to become a self-aware Muslimah who understands her inner world, knows her purpose in life, and can control her anger and pain. It means developing into a believer who can engage with others with respect and dignity, all while unapologetically loving and respecting herself. It means becoming the best version of yourself by cultivating absolute reliance on your Creator and continually course correcting when you sense yourself going astray. It means refusing to let divorce define you and understanding that you can use it as a means to earn your Creator's love. You can do all that!

Ultimately, divorce is not just an ending but also a beginning. It's a chance to rediscover yourself, to set new goals, and to create a life that aligns more closely with your true desires and values.

Embarking on this journey is not only beneficial to you; it helps your children and the coming generations as well. In healing, you are contributing to a legacy of resilience and joy. Moving forward with the lessons you learned and the strength you gained, there is hope for a brighter future.

**Go to https://www.makedayasenlul.com/divorcebookresources,
where you will find useful guides essential for Muslim moms,
including guides for achieving a purpose-driven life-work balance, starting a digital business, and more! Additionally, your
workbook is also available there.**

I would love to hear from you! Reach out to me on social media
or my website and say *salams*! Tell me about your journey or story!

Email: makeda@makedayasenlul.com

Facebook: https://www.facebook.com/profile.php?id=6155582
6318901

Instagram: https://www.instagram.com/makedayasenlul/

ACKNOWLEDGMENTS

Aisha Al Hommoud and Farrah Khan, my dear sisters and friends, you've been there with unwavering honesty through it all. You always told me what I needed to hear and kept me grounded. This book is a reflection of the wisdom you've shared with me. Your support has meant everything.

Zara J, you taught me how to trust myself, my intuition, and my dreams. You believed in me even though you found me broken.

Imam Shadeed Muhammad, Dr. Marwa Assar, and Dr. Mohammed Ghilan, your lectures brought me comfort and clarity during my divorce. Allah used your work as a means of healing for me. Keep up the great work—I'm living proof that what you do truly makes a difference.

Jamie Kern Lima and Brendon Burchard, you helped me transform my disordered understanding of self-worth into a clear and actionable roadmap.

Na'ima B. Robert, Zainab Bint Younus, and Jessica Hassan, your mentorship has been transformative. This manuscript wouldn't be what it is without your amazing support.

To all of you, thank you from the bottom of my heart. I pray that Allah rewards you in both this life and the next.

BIBLIOGRAPHY

Introduction

Brown, Brené. *The Gifts of Imperfection: Let Go of Who You Think You're Supposed to Be and Embrace Who You Are*. Hazelden, 2010.

"Divorce Among American Muslims: Statistics, Challenges, Solutions." SoundVision. Accessed July 15, 2023. https://www.soundvision.com/article/divorce-among-american-muslims-statistics-challenges-solutions.

"Understanding Divorce Rates in Muslim Communities." Farooqi and Husain. Accessed January 15, 2024. https://www.farooqihusain.com/oakbrook-terrace-lawyers/understanding-divorce-rates-in-muslim-communities.

Chapter 1

Congreve, William. *The Mourning Bride*. John Tonson, 1697.

Fisher, Helen E., Lucy L. Brown, Arthur Aron, Greg Strong, and Debra Mashek. "Reward, Addiction, and Emotion Regulation Systems Associated with Rejection in Love." *Journal of Neurophysiology* 103, no. 2 (2010): 337–47. https://journals.physiology.org/doi/full/10.1152/jn.00784.2009.

Kubler-Ross, Elisabeth. *On Death and Dying*. Scribner, 1969.

Thomas, Katherine Woodward. *Conscious Uncoupling: 5 Steps to Living Happily Even After.* Harmony Books, 2015.

"Woman Who Severed Husband's Penis Faces Life in Prison." NBC Los Angeles, June 29, 2018. https://www.nbclos angeles.com/news/local/catherine-kieu-penis-cut-off -severing-case/1953791/.

Chapter 3

Al-Ghazali, Imam. *Marvels of the Heart.* Translated by Walter James Skellie. Fons Vitae, 2010.

Al-Ghazali, Imam. *The Alchemy of Happiness.* Kazi Publications, 1991.

Al-Ghazali, Imam. *The Revival of the Religious Sciences.* Translated by Fazlul Karim. Vol. 3. Islamic Book Trust, 2015.

Makari, George. *Soul Machine: The Invention of the Modern Mind.* W. W. Norton & Company, 2015.

Martin, Howard. "Howard Martin - Engaging the Intelligence of the Heart." TedX Talks, YouTube video, January 14, 2012. https://www.youtube.com/watch?v=A9kQBAH1nK4.

Yusuf, Hamza. *Purification of the Heart: Signs, Symptoms, and Cures of the Spiritual Diseases of the Heart.* Sandala, 2012.

Chapter 5

Lima, Jamie Kern. *Worthy: How to Believe You Are Enough and Transform Your Life.* Hay House, 2024.

Chapter 7

'Terry McMillan on Letting Go of Anger." Oprah Daily. Accessed March 20, 2024. https://www.oprah.com/oprahs -lifeclass/terry-mcmillan-on-letting-go-of-anger-video.

Chapter 8

"Embracing the Shadow – Carl Jung." Orion Philosophy.
     Accessed June 20, 2024. https://orionphilosophy.com/the
     -shadow-carl-jung/.

*Muhasabah An-Nafs wal-Izra 'alayha: Holding the Soul to Account
     and Criticizing It.* Darussalam, 2022.

Tavris, Carol, and Elliot Aronson. *Mistakes Were Made (But Not
     by Me): Why We Justify Foolish Beliefs, Bad Decisions, and
     Hurtful Acts.* Harcourt, 2007.

Chapter 9

"A Guide to Istikhara: The Prayer for Guidance." Yaqeen Institute
     for Islamic Research. Accessed September 17, 2024. https://
     yaqeeninstitute.org/yaqeen-institute/a-guide-to-istikhara-the
     -prayer-for-guidance-2.

Chapter 11

"4 Ways Information Overload Impacts Our Mental Health
     and How to Cope." Mindful Health Solutions. Accessed
     July 15, 2024. https://mindfulhealthsolutions.com/4-ways
     -information-overload-impacts-our-mental-health-and-how
     -to-cope/.

"A Book a Day." Penguin Books Australia. Accessed July 15,
     2024. https://www.penguin.com.au/articles/1856-a-book
     -a-day.

"Behavioral Inhibition and the Nighttime Context." National
     Center for Biotechnology Information. Accessed July 15,
     2024. https://www.ncbi.nlm.nih.gov/pmc/articles/PMC
     9083440/.

"Brain May Flush Out Toxins During Sleep." National Institutes of Health. Accessed January 15, 2024. https://www.nih.gov/news-events/news-releases/brain-may-flush-out-toxins-during-sleep.

"Cognitive Benefits of Intermittent Fasting." National Center for Biotechnology Information. Accessed July 15, 2024. https://www.ncbi.nlm.nih.gov/pmc/articles/PMC8470960/.

"Exercising to Relax." Harvard Health Publishing. Accessed July 15, 2024. https://www.health.harvard.edu/staying-healthy/exercising-to-relax.

"Fasting and Autophagy." Spartan Medical Associates. Accessed July 15, 2024. https://www.spartanmedicalassociates.com/fasting-and-autophagy/.

Jackson-Preston, Portia. "The Missing Ingredient in Self Care | Portia Jackson-Preston | TEDxCrenshaw." TEDx Talks, YouTube video, November 5, 2019. https://www.youtube.com/watch?v=Eupk56SG76M.

"Physical Activity and Cognitive Abilities." University of Nevada. Accessed July 15, 2024. https://extension.unr.edu/publication.aspx?PubID=2921.

"Why Is the Clitoris So Sensitive? Thanks to Over 10,000 Nerves, First Real Count Finds." Medical News Today. Accessed February 5, 2024. https://www.medicalnewstoday.com/articles/why-is-the-clit-so-sensitive-thanks-to-over-10000-nerves-first-real-count-finds.

Chapter 12

Hariri, Johann. *Stolen Focus: Why You Can't Pay Attention—and How to Think Deeply Again*. Crown, 2022.

Suleiman, Omar. "The Meaning of Astaghfirullah | Ep. 5 | Deeper into Dhikr with Dr. Omar Suleiman." Yaqeen Institute, YouTube video, accessed November 11, 2024. https://www.youtube.com/watch?v=6G3FeySciwc.

Chapter 13

"5 Reasons Why Clutter Disrupts Mental Health." Psychology Today. Accessed July 15, 2024. https://www.psychologytoday .com/intl/blog/fulfillment-any-age/201705/5-reasons-why -clutter-disrupts-mental-health.

Chapter 14

Darul Ihsan Humanitarian Centre. "Life and Works of Imam Ibn Hajar Al-Asqalani (RA) – Biography." Accessed September 21, 2024. https://darulihsan.com/index.php/media1/articles /item/3346-life-and-works-of-imam-ibn-hajar-al-asqalani-ra -biography.

Muhammad, Shadeed. *The Paradox of Change: The New Muslimah's Guide to Overcoming Obstacles.* Rawdah Publishing, 2019.

Suleiman, Omar. "Umm Habiba (RA): A Dream Come True, Part 1." Yaqeen Institute for Islamic Research. Accessed September 21, 2024. https://yaqeeninstitute.org/watch/series /umm-habiba-ra-a-dream-come-true-part-1.

Suleiman, Omar. "Umm Sulaym (RA): Her Dowry Was Islam. The Firsts. Dr Omar Suleiman" Yaqeen Institute, YouTube video, February 5, 2023. https://www.youtube.com/watch ?v=2ceFscgeoPY.

Younis, Haifaa. "Mother of Imam Ahmad bin Hanbal |
    Builders of a Nation Ep. 27." Jannah Institute, YouTube
    video, February 15, 2020. https://www.youtube.com/watch
    ?v=lZbhbuo3N6Y.

ADDITIONAL RESOURCES

Please note that I have no affiliation with the resources listed below. These are either resources I have personally used and benefited from or those I have heard positive feedback about. Additionally, you will find a PDF version of this list with clickable links available at https://www.makedayasenlul.com/divorcebookresources.

Friendships | Build your village
Jackson, Danielle Bayard. *Fighting for Our Friendships: The Science and Art of Conflict and Connection in Women's Relationships.* Hachette, 2024.

Heart work | Let the heart lead the way and guide you to being in tune with yourself
Dr. Marwa Assar's The God and Me Program. https://www.thehomeinstitute.org/thegodandmeprogram/

Purpose | Live up to your full potential
Faisal Amjad's Know Your Purpose Program. https://www.kn-ow.com/kyp-program/

Psychology | Learn more about cognitive behavior

Tavris, Carol, and Elliot Aronson. *Mistakes Were Made (But Not By Me): Why We Justify Foolish Beliefs, Bad Decisions, and Hurtful Acts.* Harcourt, 2007.

Imam Shadeed Muhammad's Detox Yourself Course. https://www.rawdahislamiccenterofdelaware.com/register

Stigma | Learn historical context

Rapoport, Yossef. *Marriage, Money and Divorce in Medieval Islamic Society.* Cambridge University Press, 2015.

Phillips, Roderick. *Untying the Knot: A Short History of Divorce.* Bloomsbury, 2011.

Parenting | Control anger

McKay, Matthew, Peter Rogers, and Judith McKay. *When Anger Hurts: Quieting the Storm Within.* 2nd ed. New Harbinger Publications, 2003.

Muslim therapists, coaches, and spaces

Khalil Center. https://khalilcenter.com/

Muslim Therapists in Southern California. http://www.socalmuslimtherapists.org/

Rayesa Gheewala - The Muslimah Divorce Coach. https://www.rayesagheewala.com/

Wasilah Connections. https://wasilahconnect.org/

Looking forward | Find love again
Zara J's Captivating Courtship Coaching.
    https://captivatingcourtship.com/

Zahra Aljabri's Keys to Love Coaching.
    https://limitless.practicalmuslim.com/keys-to-love

Iffet Rafeeq's Sensual Woman Course.
    https://thebluelantern.co.uk/categories/intimacy-relationships

ABOUT THE AUTHOR

 Makeda Yasenlul is a mother, writer, and entrepreneur. Her lived experience of a challenging divorce has fueled her commitment to helping others through their own journeys, leading to the creation of *Bigger Than Divorce*.

Deeply committed to the Muslim community, Makeda believes in the power of storytelling and books as catalysts for transformation. Based in Southern California, she enjoys exploring parks, libraries, and bookstores with her daughter. Learn more at makedayasenlul.com.